IN THIS BODY,
IN THIS LIFETIME

Kannon-ji takuhatsu in the 1940s. Nagasawa Roshi is in the front.

IN THIS BODY, IN THIS LIFETIME

AWAKENING STORIES OF JAPANESE SOTO ZEN WOMEN

From Students of Sozen Nagasawa Ni-Roshi

Edited by Esho Sudan
Translated by Kogen Czarnik
Foreword by Paula Arai

SHAMBHALA

Shambhala Publications, Inc.
2129 13th Street
Boulder, Colorado 80302
www.shambhala.com

Cover art: Ekaterina/stock.adobe.com
Cover & interior design: Kate E. White

9 8 7 6 5 4 3 2 1

First Edition
Printed in the United States of America

Shambhala Publications makes every
effort to print on acid-free, recycled paper.
Shambhala Publications is distributed worldwide by
Penguin Random House, Inc., and its subsidiaries.

Library of Congress Cataloging-in-Publication Data
Names: Iizuka, Kōji, editor. | Sudan, Esho, editor. | Czarnik, Kogen, translator. | Arai,
Paula, other.
Title: In this body, in this lifetime: awakening stories of Japanese Soto Zen women from
students of Sozen Nagasawa Ni-Roshi/edited by Esho Sudan; translated by Kogen
Czarnik; foreword by Paula Arai = Sanzen taiken-shu/Koji Iizuka.
Other titles: Sanzen taiken shū. English
Description: First edition. | Boulder, Colorado: Shambhala Publications, [2025] |
Translation of: Sanzen taiken shū.—Tokyo: Chuo Bukkyo-sha, 1956. | Includes
bibliographical references. |
Identifiers: LCCN 2024041695 | ISBN 9781645473589 (trade paperback)
Subjects: LCSH: Zen meditations. | Meditation—Buddhism. | Buddhist women—Japan.
Classification: LCC BQ9289.5 .S2613 2025 | DDC 294.3/927092520952—
dc23/eng/20241104
LC record available at https://lccn.loc.gov/2024041695

The authorized representative in the EU for product safety and compliance is eucomply
OÜ, Pärnu mnt 139b-14, 11317 Tallinn, Estonia, hello@eucompliancepartner.com.

Contents

Foreword

We know that women have been active since the inception of the Buddhist tradition. Across centuries and a wide range of cultures, they have deeply immersed themselves in and carried forward innumerable schools of Buddhist thought and practice and have stimulated new approaches to practice. Yet we have precious few historical records that detail what they thought and did, at least beyond the fact that they were successful in nurturing a tradition that now spans the world and has continued for twenty-five hundred years to offer direction to those aching to stop suffering.

In This Body, In This Lifetime gives us access to intimate moments that thirty Japanese women experienced as they were taken under the powerful wings of a ferociously compassionate female Zen master, Sozen Nagasawa Roshi. Primarily in the aftermath of World War II, she midwifed lay and monastic women through the painful journey that opened each of them up to the liberating joy and gratitude of living *Mu*. In this book, you witness the power of the teacher through the depth the disciples go to break through. The intensity of pain and anguish the women endured to be released from dualistic delusions is palpable through the vulnerability and raw honesty they courageously share. Their stories overflow with tears and repentance. Doubts of self-worth leak through. Reliance on others—including ancestors, buddhas, and bodhisattvas, especially Kannon—is resolute.

I am a scholar and practitioner of Japanese Buddhism, and the writings you hold in your hands overlap with the period I covered in my volume *Women Living Zen*. Yet this book provides a fuller and deeper picture of Soto Zen nuns and laywomen. The personal stories of these women, largely unknown beyond a core circle of Japanese Soto Zen women, are humbling. They reveal the immensity of their lives through the severity and profound earnestness of their commitment. Their stories are written like spiritual diary entries that illuminate their hard-won wisdom. Through them, the magnitude of Nagasawa Roshi's wisdom and compassion radiates.

Listen to the chorus of voices that, through this translation, can now reverberate into the hearts of English readers.

If you cannot take on the suffering of the Great Universe, you will not attain the happiness of the Great Universe either.
—*Rev. Kanko Ishimoto*

Don't be wary of people. Become a person who can take anyone into her heart. This is what it means to be a peaceful person.
—*Nagasawa Roshi counsels Ms. Aiko Nakano*

Wash your whole body and mind with those tears and come back.
—*Nagasawa Roshi advises Rev. Zenkai Yamauchi*

But now my body and mind have become light, and I know that helping others means you must forget yourself and dive into the state of mind of that person, becoming one with their joy and their suffering.
—*Rev. Setsujo Uchiyama*

My feelings for the Venerable Abbess are just like those of a baby toward her mother. With love she is teaching and fostering us like a parent who teaches their child to crawl, stand, and walk. And I am determined to wholeheartedly continue making a diligent effort.

—Ms. Moto Yamada, laywoman who
raised two sons that returned from war

Even such a wretch as me could penetrate *Mu*.

—Rev. Tokuo Ito

I realized, *This "me" who is practicing, this is Buddha!* As soon as I thought that, a waterfall of tears started to flow. . . . I cried and cried, my tears filling the whole heaven and earth. . . . I aspire not to neglect my daily life, not to waste it, to be a good wife and a good mother, to strongly continue to grow, and to be a person of true virtue.

—Ms. Chiyo Ikai

Searching for this truth, one must confess everything and make one's mind totally honest.

—Rev. Gyokusen Tanimori

Ah, the world of the Way is strict, but this strictness is filled with the taste of inexpressible warmth, boundless vastness, depth, wisdom, and compassion.

—Rev. Hogaku Shibutani

The bright green fields of barley look brave. Bathed in the spring sun, they are burning with hope.

—Rev. Sosen Koide

May the wisdom of the monastic and lay disciples of Nagasawa Roshi resound into our world and inspire generations to come, especially those who harbor self-doubt and face intractable challenges.

Paula Arai

Translator's Introduction

In most religions, every several generations, an outstanding teacher appears and revitalizes their tradition. Kojun Sozen Nagasawa Roshi (1888–1971) was such a figure for Zen Buddhist nuns in twentieth-century Japan. However, she remains largely unknown in the West, despite being the only independently teaching female Zen master of her time, a reformer who played a major role in the fight to gain equal rights for nuns, and a powerful spiritual guide for generations of women as well as men.

The girl who would become Sozen Nagasawa Roshi was born as Tora Nagasawa in 1888, and from a young age she longed to become a nun. In her own words, "The original cause for me to become a monastic was when I first saw a nun. I was seven years old. In the province I was born in, there were no nuns. But one day, there was a nun who was traveling from a distant province to Bodai-ji temple, and she stayed for one night [in our town]. I saw her just for a moment, but this became a reason for me to have affinity with the Dharma. From then on, I couldn't stop wishing to become a nun until this vow was realized." She wasn't able to fulfill her aspiration for some time, as her parents were opposed to the idea. Respecting their wishes, she went to a teacher training college and began a career in education.

When Sozen Roshi was twenty-seven, her parents died, and she started to think again of her original aspiration. Still, those around her were not supportive. As Sozen Roshi recalls, "I was told . . . that there are no more useless people than nuns, that becoming a nun is nothing I should consider. Truly, I heard it so many times that it almost made my ears develop a callous . . . yet I was drawn to great ideals, and I wanted to live in a pure world. Putting my life on the line, I became a nun."[1]

She received ordination in 1915 from Daiun Sogaku Harada Roshi, one of the most prominent teachers in the Soto school in the first half of the twentieth century. However, Sogaku Roshi was still a lecturer at the Soto school's Komazawa University at the time and didn't have his own training temple where she could go to practice. There was also not a single practice monastery for nuns in the Soto school, only a few newly established seminaries (Jap. *gakurin*) mostly focused on secular and vocational education, like the one in Nagoya, Aichi prefecture (which several decades later became Aichi Senmon Ni-Sodo) and in Koide, Niigata, where Sozen Roshi went to receive basic monastic education. There was no zazen practice in the seminary; so, searching for more authentic training after she graduated, she went to Enko-ji in Kyoto, the only training nunnery of the Rinzai school at the time. The nunnery had an abbess and daily zazen practice, but the Dharma teachings were given by a male teacher from a nearby monastery.

In 1920, Sogaku Roshi recommended that Sozen Roshi train under Shoin Yamashina Roshi at the Rinzai school's Shogen-ji training monastery. Known as "the peerless demon's dojo" for its rigorous practice, Shogen-ji was where Sogaku Roshi himself had trained as a young monk. It was a men-only monastery, and only through a personal connection of Sogaku Harada Roshi was she allowed to train there. It was a very challenging thing to do in the patriarchal society of Japan a hundred years ago. That same year,

Sozen Roshi had her first *kensho*, or awakening experience. After Shoin Roshi died, Sozen Roshi continued to train with his successor, Isei Kominami Roshi, until a serious illness forced her to leave Shogen-ji.[2]

Speaking of her training, Sozen Roshi would later say, "At the time, there was no suitable practice monastery for nuns, so enduring various hardships I was going here and there, and how many times this body was at the verge of death. The golden and unsurpassed words of buddhas and ancestors were penetrating my bones and marrow, and I didn't have time to spare to listen to the worldly ways of criticizing nuns. When I thought, *Thankfully, I am also a Dharma descendant of all buddhas of the three worlds*, I just wanted to advance in my practice. I wanted to practice with other nuns and laywomen who had a precious affinity with the Dharma."[3]

By the time Sozen Roshi recovered from her illness, Sogaku Harada Roshi had left Komazawa University and become the abbot of Hosshin-ji monastery in the town of Obama, Fukui prefecture. Sozen Roshi went to continue her practice with him there, completing koan training under him and receiving *shiho* (Dharma transmission) and *inka shomei* (authorization to teach) from him. In 1935, she left to establish a training monastery for nuns near Tokyo—and thus began Kannon-ji in Mitaka, Tokyo prefecture, the only practice place in the entire Zen tradition, at the time, where a nun was the spiritual leader.

Sozen Roshi wrote, "As I am a nun, I have wished for over twenty years to create a place primarily for nuns, where women who are determined to practice can gather and do this great training. Finally I was able to establish this temple, albeit humble in appearance, like a pig pen. It is strange, or rather miraculous, that while we are poor, we are lucky to be able to walk toward our ideals, thanks to the divine protection of the buddhas and heavens."[4]

Sozen Roshi began teaching in a small building, without any temple supporters. The practice place was maintained mostly through the mendicant practice known in Japanese as *takuhatsu*, which is very unusual in Japan—most temples rely primarily on temple members for their income. Through great determination and hardship, Sozen Roshi gathered enough resources to build a new main temple hall, meditation hall, and kitchen building[5] in a location near the original site. Soon Kannon-ji became a well-known training monastery for women, where entire generations of nuns could train with a female teacher, realize their true nature, and, after leaving, help others in any capacity to which they felt called. Many of her students returned to their home temples and wanted to help nuns and laywomen in their areas to have the same opportunity they had had to meet with true teachings. In various parts of the country, these nuns organized *sesshins* and shorter retreats with zazen, lectures, and guidance from Sozen Roshi, who tirelessly continued to give her entire life to teaching, until her death in 1971.

Like Kannon Bodhisattva with thirty-three faces, Sozen Roshi taught her students in a variety of ways—sometimes with grandmotherly kindness, and sometimes with a strict and fierce style meant to push her students beyond their limitations. All of the stories in this book describe the experience of practice under her guidance, especially during weeklong intensive retreats. In almost all cases, Sozen Roshi would assign students a breath-counting meditation to help them gain basic stability of mind. Later, she would give them a breakthrough koan called Joshu's Dog, or the *Mu* koan. The koan says, "A monk asked Joshu, 'Does a dog have Buddha-nature?' Joshu said, 'No (*Mu*).'" On each exhalation, the student repeats this one syllable, "*Mu*," as a *wato* (lit. "word head"), putting all their energy and longing for liberation into it. Through this practice, they unify body and mind and enter samadhi, becoming *Mu*, until a breakthrough occurs, bringing about a realization of the true nature of mind (kensho). This process happens in the context of an ongoing teacher-student relationship and under guidance in one-on-one meetings called *dokusan*. Although from the Meiji era the use of koans and guidance through dokusan started to disappear in the Soto school, Sozen Roshi trained in the lineage where that was not the case (as well as in the Rinzai school) and successfully lead many women to liberative insights using those practices.

To empower other nuns—and, even more importantly, laywomen, who often were led to wrongly believe that such an insight was out of their reach by the religious establishment— whenever Sozen Roshi verified the kensho of one of her students, she asked them to write down their experience, together with a short background story that would describe how they had reached it. *Mahayana Zen*, a Buddhist magazine of the Chuo Bukkyo-sha publishing house, then printed the reports. By the mid-1950s, there were so many stories that the publisher chose sixty to release in book form, titled *Sanzen taiken-shu* (*Collection of Experiences in Zen Practice*). This was the original publication on which *In This Body, In This Lifetime* is based.

It is worth noting that although the practice under a female Zen master with a female sangha was different in some ways from that of monks' monasteries, it is clear that Sozen Roshi's approach was no less strict or intense. One major difference is that practitioners were allowed and often encouraged to do their practice aloud when sitting—either counting the breath or practicing the koan *Mu*. This is rarely the case in a Zen monastery. Sozen Roshi's teacher, Sogaku Harada Roshi, would sometimes allow his students to practice aloud in the last period of evening zazen during retreats, and he would encourage it during outdoors night sitting, but at Kannon-ji, most people were told to practice aloud all the time. What may also surprise the reader is the extent to which prayer and devotion to buddhas and bodhisattvas was emphasized as a necessary component of practice, contrary to the popular belief sometimes found in the West that Zen is done on one's own, without a devotional aspect.

Additionally, Kannon-ji was not as strict with the rule of silence during retreat as other Zen temples were, though it is clear in these accounts that silence was broken only for the purposes of mutual encouragement between practitioners. Outside of the strict three-month *ango* (practice period) at Kannon-ji, nuns would sometimes hold celebrations around a bonfire where they would perform traditional Japanese dances. They also ran an orphanage, taking care of children who had lost their parents during World War II.

Sozen Roshi was not just a formidable teacher; she also played a key role in the struggle for nuns to be given equal rights in the Soto school. Nuns had always received far less support than monks, both from the Soto school organization and society in general. They were not allowed to study at the Soto school's Komazawa University, and, most importantly, they were not allowed to give Dharma transmission (an authorization to teach) to their students, even if they had received one from a male teacher. This prohibition prevented nuns from having their own female lineage. Sozen Roshi, together with Rev. Kendo Kojima, a Soto school nun who trained under Sozen Roshi at Kannon-ji and whose story is recounted in this volume (see page 29), traveled throughout Japan, organizing and gathering support for the Soto School's Nuns Association (established in the mid-1940s) and the National Organization of Nuns (established in 1951). Sozen Roshi was the vice president of both these groups, yet her primary focus remained on teaching and leading retreats and training nuns at Kannon-ji. Finally, during the seven-hundredth anniversary of the death of Dogen Zenji, the founder of the Japanese Soto school, in 1952, a new amendment was passed in the Soto school constitution, allowing nuns to give Dharma transmission.

By the time Sozen Nagasawa Roshi passed away in 1971, she had raised generations of nuns who later led practice meetings in their own temples. She wrote the book *Keys to Zen Training for Women*[6] and helped to create *Collection of Experiences in Zen Training*. Her legacy includes a thriving nunnery run by nuns for nuns and at least three successors to whom she was able to legally pass her Dharma transmission because of the changes to the Soto school constitution that she had helped to bring about. The aim of this book is to introduce Western Dharma practitioners to Sozen Nagasawa Roshi's great legacy.

The intention behind making this translation was for Sozen Nagasawa Roshi's teachings to become a source of inspiration for practitioners today, encouraging them to follow the example of the brave Dharma practitioners in these pages. There are two elements of great importance in Zen practice: one is the guidance of a realized teacher, and the second is the sincere practice of the students. This book is a testimony to the power that is unlocked when those two components come together. All the women whose stories are presented in this book—regardless of obstacles and adversity—believed that attaining deep realization is possible for everyone. They searched for a true Dharma teacher, followed her guidance, and awakened to their true nature. May the merit of this work benefit all beings and contribute to the continuity of the Buddhadharma.

Kogen Czarnik
May 2024
Bukkoku-ji

Editor's Note

When I entered a Soto Japanese training monastery as a Western female monastic in Okayama in 2010, I rarely encountered Japanese nuns. It seemed there was only one in the entire prefecture at that time. Laywomen were also few and far between, although they did come to the monastery to attend ceremonies, cook, sew, make tea, arrange flowers, or weed, but rarely to practice.

Through the one Soto nun of Okayama, I learned that there are still nuns and nunneries in Japan today, most notably the Aichi Senmon Ni-Sodo run by Abbess Shundo Aoyama Roshi in Nagoya. I also learned that although they still practice zazen and sesshin, academic studies and "temple arts" are a large part of the curriculum, to provide the nuns with a livelihood in a system where most temples are handed down from father to son.

How remarkable it was, then, to discover in the out-of-print text *Collection of Experiences in Zen Training* that there was a powerful female teacher—namely, Sozen Nagasawa Roshi—who, in the challenging conditions of wartime Japan, established a women's monastery solely for the purpose of Dharma practice and awakening, without receiving the support her male counterparts did.

Her name appears in the list of female ancestors sometimes chanted in Western Zen centers, yet there is very little known about her. What makes this text so significant is that it may well be the only record of a female Zen master teaching independently in Japan, until Nagasawa Roshi trailblazed a path for other women to teach and transmit their lineages with full authority. Before Nagasawa Roshi, the historic women we encounter in the Japanese Zen tradition are students of notable male teachers, or they appear as patrons and supporters or as bit parts in Zen stories. But here Nagasawa Roshi is described as the primary spiritual guide—firsthand, in action—by the many students she brought to awakening. Working on this text has been an intimate, transformative experience, like being able to listen in on and witness in real time teachings being given to these laywomen and nuns, as though I were sitting in the zendo right alongside them.

Nagasawa Roshi's students included farmers' wives, grieving mothers, and temple daughters—women who would never have had access to such teaching otherwise. These women sat at first in a space barely larger than a "pigpen," as Sozen Roshi described it. They continued to sit in zazen while Tokyo was being bombed. And they survived the hardship of postwar, near starvation, by giving to those in greater need around them, all the while never wavering in their commitment to the real purpose of a Zen nun's being: to awaken oneself and others.

The original collection of stories numbered sixty. The thirty collected here were selected to give a sense of the diversity of women—of all classes, ages, and life situations—who practiced under Sozen Roshi's guidance. (It is important to note that men also came to Nagasawa Roshi for spiritual instruction, and some of their stories were in the original collection.) Many of these women had little access to education, so it was necessary to modify some of the original text for readability—for example, revising the sequence of sentences for chronological order. We also reordered some of the chapters to allow the text to flow better as a whole. May the authors forgive us these liberties.

As these narratives can include many locations, some clarification is needed on the differences in the temple environments these women were moving between. The nuns were usually ordained in local temples in which they lived and worked alongside an older abbess, until they succeeded her. Often they attended for some years a nuns' seminary, which was the only educational and vocational training available to them. Finally, there was Kannon-ji, the temple in Tokyo that Nagasawa Roshi established as the first women's monastery to be entirely focused on zazen and sesshin practice, in 1935. Most of the nuns later returned from Kannon-ji to their home temples, offering teachings and zazen instruction to the local community. One such place was Chido-an in Nigori-kawa, Niigata prefecture, where Nagasawa Roshi often conducted sesshins. The nuns in these stories uniformly express that it wasn't until they practiced together under Sozen Nagasawa Roshi, among their Dharma sisters, that they truly understood the meaning of the life they had taken up.

Kannon-ji, currently run by a nun in Nagasawa Roshi's lineage, is still a place of women's practice, although it is skeletally staffed now, having suffered the same fate as other monasteries and temples in an increasingly secular Japan.

Given this context, discovering the presence of such a formidable and powerful female ancestor teaching direct awakening in my own Soto school has been particularly moving. Perhaps most moving of all is to encounter the way in which Nagasawa Roshi clearly transcends gender and nationality altogether, to embody and teach a truth beyond all relative expression.

Westerners, and especially Western women, training in Soto Zen in Japan today often observe that they still face inequality. And Japanese monks and nuns would most likely agree that direct teachings on realization and awakening are rare. And yet Nagasawa Roshi's life and teaching remind us that there have always been people who refuse to let their circumstances obstruct the truth—people whose influence as living examples affected not only individual women and men, lay and ordained, but a whole wisdom tradition in which the awakened mind can still be transmitted and verified, down to this day. May the editing of this text be a humble offering toward that end.

Esho Sudan
June 2024
Tosho-ji

IN THIS BODY,
IN THIS LIFETIME

Nagasawa Roshi in 1939.

Original Preface

One time, Shakyamuni Buddha told his disciple Ananda, "Take a pinch of dirt from the ground and put it on your fingernail. Among all creatures born in this world, those born as human beings can be compared to the amount of dirt on your fingernail, and those born as other beings, to the amount of soil in the great earth." Then he continued, "Ananda, among all beings born as human beings in this world, those people who are able to encounter the Buddhadharma can be compared to the amount of dirt on your fingernail, and those unable to encounter the Buddhadharma, to the amount of soil in the great earth. You have been blessedly born as a human being, and were able to meet with this precious Buddhadharma, therefore you should heedfully practice."[7] That was the teaching he gave.

In the *Shushogi* we read, "It is difficult to be born as a human being; it is rare to encounter the Buddhadharma. Now, thanks to our good deeds in the past, not only have we been born as humans, [but] we have also encountered the Buddhadharma. Within the realm of birth and death, this good birth is the best."[8] For human beings, there is no higher meaning in life than encountering the Buddhadharma; saving oneself, saving others, and establishing a world of truth.

All of the Dharma friends who wrote this *Collection of Experiences in Zen Practice* had their fair share of suffering and discovered the true value of life. If these stories can be at all helpful for readers, I would be truly grateful.

Under the heavens, till the end, end, end of all fields,
Long-awaited fresh breeze of the Dharma.

August 1956, Kannon-ji
Sozen Nagasawa

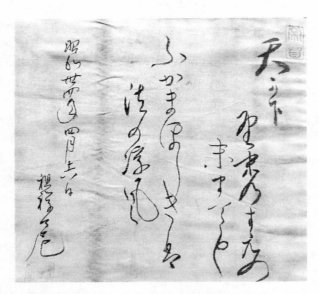

Calligraphy of the translated poem above by Nagasawa Roshi;
written on the reverse side of a rakusu.

Tora Nagasawa, ca. 1908.

Ordination picture of Sozen Kojun Nagasawa Roshi, ca. 1915.

Nagasawa Roshi (left) during work practice at Enko-ji, ca. 1919.

Nagasawa Roshi (fourth from the left) at Hosshin-ji with her ordination teacher, Daiun Sogaku Harada Roshi (center), ca. 1930.

STORIES OF AWAKENING

Early days of Kannon-ji, ca. 1935, Nagasawa Roshi on the left.

1

REMEMBERING MY CHILD

Ms. Momoyo Nakayama

I LOST IN THE WAR my beloved only son, for whom there is no replacement in heaven or on earth. Just three days after graduating from Tokyo Imperial University, he left for the front in high spirits to serve as a reservist. In the Philippines, the lifetime of this mere sapling of twenty-six was ended.

Cultivating his parents' fields—his father's as a person of religion, and his mother's as an educator—he wrote his final thesis on *The Place of High Priest Myoe in the History of Education.*[9] From an early age he had idealized his ordinary parents, and his hope was to inherit the kindergarten that I ran and to become a religious educator. He was concerned for the happiness of young children, and he was devoted to his mother. His greater purpose, as a true man of religion, was to serve all people of the world, extending to the Way itself, revering all buddhas and ancestors. He was a son we could only have dreamed of, an ideal human being; and it was I—usually raising and guiding children—who was all the time taught and purified by him. I wondered how this child could have come from my womb, having been born and raised by such a sinful mother as me. I thought I must have become his mother by mistake.

From kindergarten and into my son's school days, everybody who knew him loved his friendly and generous character, and they grieved at the news of his death. A wounded soldier who had served under my son and had miraculously survived returned and visited me after the war. Kneeling before our home altar, with hands in *gassho* (gesture of putting palms together) and tears in his eyes, he told me, "He was truly a kind commander. He loved his subordinates, and no matter what happened, he never reprimanded us. In other units, the commander would eat his food first, but our commander would give food to us first. Therefore, all of us adored him and trusted him. In the last moments, although we knew there was no hope, and we were told that we could stop fighting, every single one of us wanted to share the fate of the commander. I was wounded in the chest, but I told him I wanted to go on with him. Unusually, he got angry and said, 'Just dying is not thinking about our country and showing gratitude to our parents. You are young, and your wound will certainly heal, so take responsibility for the seriously wounded, and take them to the back for me.' Then he put in order the lucky charms he had received from you, and your photographs, and threw away the commander's sword he had been carrying, saying, 'Because we create things like this, it all goes wrong!' Then, unarmed, he calmly walked toward the enemy's position. This is what I have to say to you, his mother."

May 7, 1945, was a day I won't ever be able to forget. It is when I received the remains of my son's body, returned ceremonially, with the news of his death in war. I cannot express the grief and anguish I felt when I held in my arms this small box made of plain wood, even in such words as "I felt like vomiting blood" or "I was in heartrending grief." Only other mothers who have experienced this can know the feeling.

From a world of light, I was thrown into a world of darkness. I lost all desire to live. All my happiness was taken away. I had devoted my life to raising this son, often alone, as my husband was a foreign missionary, absent for long periods in a temple in Hawaii. I had taken such delight in my beloved child's growth. For him to reach adulthood was my one great goal, the only light and hope of my life. Whatever pains and sorrows that arose along the way amounted to nothing—my life had been vibrant like an always full moon. Now I lived in grief, empty like a soulless puppet, devastated by the loss of my child, grieving day and night. I don't know how many times I thought to follow my beloved child into death, but each time when I was about to do it, I would clearly hear his dear voice saying, "Mom, you must not die. Please be happy. Please live in happiness."

My son didn't want me to suffer or die. I just had to cry until it was enough. People criticized me as a foolish mother, a prisoner of my emotions. I had fallen as low as one can. In the morning and the evening I would make a ceremonial food offering, chant a sutra, and offer incense and flowers before his spirit. This brought me some consolation, but I continued in this wretched state day and night for over three years. I had taught over two thousand children and had guided many young mothers, but now my life was in a pitiful state.

Finally, I met Sozen Nagasawa Roshi of Kannon-ji, the nuns' training monastery, and listened to one of her talks. At first I thought, *How could a nun who has never given birth or raised a child, let alone had her child be killed, ever understand this pain, this suffering? There is no one in this world I can turn to.* My heart remained shut tight. However, as I listened to her, I was deeply moved by her character. There was some untouchable intensity about her. At the same time, she had a childlike innocence that pulled me toward her. I thought, *She is different from the other nuns I have met so far.* I was gradually drawn in more and more by her lectures and started to think maybe I would give zazen a try.

I went at first for two days of sesshin, then three days, and finally I completed a whole seven-day sesshin. As one retreat followed another, my own foolishness keenly sunk into my mind. I realized that although Roshi didn't have the experience of giving birth to a child, raising him, and having him die, from the perspective of practice, she possessed exalted experience surpassing that of the mothers of the world. She was strict and fierce, and yet the shining light of her great compassion guided this community—composed of very different people—with complete mastery. This was the true mind of compassion! I resolved that I would train under her and break through the ultimate barrier.

From then on, I pushed forward in a literal do-or-die struggle, relying entirely on Roshi. However, I soon discovered breaking through is easier said than done. During sesshin, the suffering, sorrow, anxiety, and misery I experienced were beyond words. People who haven't done this kind of retreat cannot imagine or know the agony of it. I jumped into this world of practice as a beginner, not knowing anything about it. Initially I was completely surprised. When the assembly started to earnestly intone *Mu* out loud, I thought it was ridiculous, that maybe I had walked into a mental hospital and this was a gathering of the insane.

Meals were another surprise. How many times did we reverently put our hands in gassho? We did it when we received two slices of pickled radish, or the rice gruel, or the water for the cleaning of the bowls, and so on. For the whole meal it seemed there was no break from holding our hands in gassho. There was beauty, harmony, and grace in this solemn way of eating, but it was accompanied by a sense of rigidity and tautness.

In the pursuit of *Mu* I didn't change my meditation posture and I didn't sleep. I lost sensation in my whole body from the pain in my legs, and sparks would fly out of my eyes. Even as I was in a continuous struggle that felt like a thousand deaths and a million hardships, without any mercy, I was hit hard from behind.

It was the first time in my life that I had ever been hit by someone, and in that instant I thought, *How barbaric!* My resistant mind started to heat up, and I went to dokusan furious and crying. "Don't try to argue! It's just your ego attachment!" the Abbess roared, and she chased me away with the ringing of her bell.

Mu-, Mu-, Mu-! I grappled with *Mu* with all my might. But even while I was desperately putting my life on the line, I would just hear, "That's just emotion!" "That's an excuse!" "That's an explanation!" "What are you dawdling over?" As I was scolded thoroughly, my beliefs and ideas were being destroyed. *Mu-, Mu-, Mu-!*—whether sleeping or during the meal, while in the toilet— only *Mu-, Mu-, Mu-!*

With the passage of time, I lost my appetite. I couldn't sleep at night, and I just sat up in meditation, the exhaustion of my body and mind reaching an extreme. During *kinhin* (walking meditation), I couldn't take even a single step. I was seized by *Mu*, tormented by *Mu*. I was crying out *Mu*, yet I could not grasp *Mu*. During dokusan I was told, "That's *makyo* (hallucination)!" "That's belief!" "That's an idea!" "Don't intoxicate yourself with Dharma joy!" It was an unbearable, ruthless, sharp whip of words. I had exhausted all means, and I had nothing to hang on to. Thrown down and sunk to the very bottom, I felt that there was no hope for me anymore and that I was a sinful person completely without the right to be saved. I even thought, *My son disappeared with the dew on the battlefield, but his anguish couldn't be worse than his mother's is now.*

Sometimes, in my ignorance and in vain hope, I relied on Roshi—a true teacher of the Way—to save me. Other times I just wanted to run from the temple as fast as I could. Once I went to my room crying, even packing my bags—when from the very bottom of my heart a voice came, saying, *Under the skies of a foreign country far from his motherland, without anything to drink or to eat, hiding in the fields, sleeping in the mountains, how many times did my son dream of his hometown? Surely he wanted to see his father and mother and his beloved only sister. What was the state of mind of this child of mine who died a noble death? He cut off the self-interest that is so difficult to sever and knew the preciousness of life while having no way to go forward and, if that was his superiors' orders, no way to retreat—I must think of my child's death in battle! What is my suffering in comparison? It is not even anything worth mentioning. If I, his mother, won't realize the Way now, when will my dead son and I ever be saved from this world?* Instantly the intention to run away vanished, and with great inspiration and renewed courage, I continued my practice.

Until then I had been trapped, enclosed in a narrow and hard shell, unable to move. With the progress of the practice my self-centeredness started to recede. And freed from distracting thoughts, gradually I was able to break out into an expansive, bright world. From the bottom of my heart I could prostrate myself in gratitude for a single slice of pickled radish, one grain of rice in the gruel, or even the intense whip.

As the wife of a priest, I had eaten Buddha's food, I had been taught the Dharma and read Buddhist books, and it seemed I had grasped it theoretically. But now I was ashamed, and I couldn't bear the remorse. I was made painfully aware that unless I endured the hardships of practice and really experienced awakening myself, in a time of crisis, it was all of no use. This really soaked into the marrow of my bones.

Encouraged, I went to dokusan, but once again I was told, "You're just finding Dharmic pleasure in the world of faith! Why are you so stingy? Come out! Come out! Come and grasp *Mu*. Don't hesitate! Reveal yourself completely. Come out and grasp it! Come on! Come on!" Sitting face to face, the Abbess kept poking me with the *kyosaku* (wooden stick). There was nothing I could hold on to. What agony!

Here where I find myself, there is only death . . . it is death, it is Mu, it is death, it is Mu, it is Mu, it is Mu! Forget about dokusan! Mu-, Mu-, Mu-! There is only Mu! I went out into the garden and quietly sat. In front of the temple there was a large tree, almost reaching to the clouds. Harmonizing with my *Mu-, Mu-, Mu-!*, the tree was making the earth tremble, urging me on. All the flowers and every single azalea leaf were talking to me. At night, the brilliant moon became one with me, laughing.

Morning came. How pleasant was the morning practice, how clear the little bird's song was! The sound of the cutting board of the temple's cook was so crisp—*chop, chop, chop.* The sound of the mallet of the elderly lady living behind the temple cracking open soybean pods—everything was an exquisite piece of music that no words in the world could describe. *I guess this is what it means to go to the Pure Land, the greatest joy,* I thought. There was no longer the troublesome *Saha* world (world of suffering), nor was there the Venerable Abbess. The clinging to my beloved dead son had disappeared, as had the painful pursuit of *Mu,* in this samadhi of Dharma joy.

However, once again, I was startled by the roar of the Abbess, and a *Whack! Whack! Whack!* of the stick. I was instructed to return to *Mu.* Again, *Mu-, Mu-, Mu-!* A tiny bug landing on the paper screen; it was *Mu.* An airplane flying through the sky; it was *Mu.* The whole universe was nothing but *Mu.* The paper screen in front of me started to dissolve, and I couldn't see anymore. My body felt as if it were being pulled into the deep bottom of the earth.

When the *bonsho* (temple bell) rang, in that instant, suddenly, I broke through! I realized that heaven and earth are one; myself and the universe are one body. Buddha is what I am! There is only unity. Everything is *Mu*. This great treasure I grasped has not even a gap for a feather to pass through. No one could ever harm it—it transcends even death. The Venerable Abbess herself could not damage or destroy it.

It is perfect, it is perfect, it is perfect. Even the Venerable Abbess probably didn't reach this far, I thought, and I was finally able to go to dokusan as the original self, imperturbable. For the first time, the Venerable Abbess smiled warmly and approved my experience. Then she gave me various guidelines and cautions.

My joy disappeared as I was made aware of the responsibility and trials of a person aspiring to the Way. Now I deeply understood the words of encouragement the Venerable Abbess had been telling me: "Don't intoxicate yourself with Dharma joy." I was presented with another koan to further refine my state of mind.

Compared to how I had been living—inside the narrow, hard shell of my own suffering—this is a different world. And although it is a path of trials, and the adversities one has to overcome to reach the state of mind of all buddhas and ancestors are immeasurable, actually walking this path is the greatest joy.

The timeless, indestructible life is continuously bestowing me with each moment. Here, living and working together with my dead son is a joy that cannot be expressed in words. This is the Buddha-mind, that is the Buddha-mind—there is nothing that is not the Buddha-mind. This is joy, that is delight. My life is complete and overflowing in this fresh, pure, vast heaven and earth. During a lecture, Roshi said,

> Like a clear dew,
> my mind
> if placed on an autumn leaf
> just as it is—a ruby.

When my mind is colorless and transparent, no matter what circumstances arise, I can adapt to them. I have started a new life, a life worth living, where with each step I am repaying the kindness of buddhas and ancestors. And while I won't ever be able to forget the austerities of sesshin, I have only the deepest gratitude for all the troubles that the Venerable Abbess took to teach me. I can only put my hands together in gassho.

2

GREAT DHARMA RAIN

Rev. Shoho Kojima

THE WAR STARTED when I was in elementary school. I grew up at a time when we were completely focused on the protection of our country. When we lost the war, I was seventeen. Back then, when I was looking at the world of adults, I felt gloomy about the future. *Why do people of the world have to hurt each other?* I wondered. *I am a nun, and nuns should be noble, but is there really a noble nun in this world? And if so, where?* All monastics seemed to be just pandering to society for the sake of their livelihood.

When I would witness this reality, I felt happy that at least I was not corrupt, but I had no idea what on earth I should do. Living as a monastic, relying on the offerings of faithful people, is a great responsibility, and I felt an unbearable sense of inferiority. Talking to my Dharma friends, everyone was suffering. Our young hearts, left without any guidance, were infected with postwar nihilism. We graduated from the nuns' seminary without any resolution to our deep questions. All my Dharma friends went back to their respective temples, and I was thrown into society.

I had an interest in childcare, so I became a kindergarten teacher. The young children were innocent and full of hope and learning how to care for them was delightful. This revived me, and for a while I aspired to become a good teacher and give my all for the sake of society. Soon I became the head of a kindergarten, but when bowing to the Buddha together with the children, I realized I didn't know what Buddha was. I would touch my shaved head and, even though I was a monastic, I felt like a fake. *What in the world am I doing?* I wondered. Me talking about the Buddha to the young children seemed meaningless, and that old feeling came back to me again: *Is there no one who can teach me?*

I began to search in desperation. Whenever I was happy that I had finally found a true teacher, in the end all they could give me were perfunctory sermons. Just when I really didn't know what to do with my hollow body and mind, one evening, when I was going to sleep at my home temple, from behind the paper screen I heard a voice say, "The young nuns that left the seminary all seem to be suffering, poor things. . . . " I was surprised and stood up from my bed, even forgetting to put on my robes. In the room next door, the Venerable Abbess of Kannon-ji nunnery in Mitaka was talking to my ordination teacher, saying, "It's because they don't know the true Dharma . . . " I listened intently. These words, heard for the first time, captivated me and took my anguish away, just by hearing them. Soon after that, surmounting many difficulties, I entered Kannon-ji, the nun's monastery, for training.

To have found a place in this world where that kind of beautiful life can be lived among so many people burning with desire to progress on the path—I was so grateful and happy. I practiced the koan Joshu's *Mu* and did a few sesshins. For me, to whom thoughts of self-doubt clung, becoming simpleminded was extraordinarily difficult.

My evil karma would make a display every sesshin, and I would continue to repent. The embarrassment of failing, sesshin after sesshin, was so bitter. I felt like I could not make a dent in this thing called kensho. I was tormented by inexpressible anxiety. Although I was trying everything, I was confronted with my inability to dive in deeply. I was stuck in every direction.

Nonetheless, when the November sesshin finished, all the usual stubborn thoughts had vanished, and I was able to obediently listen to what everyone was telling me. I realized that making an effort to cultivate myself was the most delightful thing I could do in this world, and I completely devoted myself to worshipping the Buddha and to sitting.

One day, when we went to Asakusabashi for takuhatsu, I saw a dead person tied with a rope and pulled by a boat in the river. It was the most pitiable sight I had ever seen in my life. Death!!! How many hundreds of times before had I heard that humans inevitably die. I thought I knew this truth. But suddenly it became clear: I also will die. And for the first time, I knew a great fear. *The pitiable sight of this dead man is how I will look tomorrow. I don't even really know if there is tomorrow. This is dreadful.* It was as if someone had hit me with a club. Spontaneously, the practice started to flow out of me—*Mu-, Mu-, Mu-!*—I wanted somehow to escape this fear of death. *All the people walking by me are all heading toward death. I have to save all of them!* The Venerable Abbess was always saying, "To guide others to the world of peace, we have to first become ourselves a peaceful person." I felt that no matter what, I had to awaken as fast as possible. *For that, there is absolutely no other way than penetrating Mu.* A cold sweat was pouring down my back, and I had the feeling I was being chased by something. Ghastly pale, I returned to the temple.

The time for *rohatsu* sesshin (annual intensive retreat commemorating the Buddha's enlightenment) came. I firmly believed that if I sincerely practiced *Mu*, I would not fail. I entreated the buddhas and ancestors to help me, but from the third day, I started to get absent-minded again. My leg pain was only getting worse. I began to bow and repent: *All the bad karma created by me in the past* . . . The dead person I had seen at the river and I became one, the image of one death flashing before my eyes.

Around the fourth day, during dokusan, suddenly all the surroundings turned into *Mu*. *Mu* flooded my whole body. Surprised, I tried to grasp it, but it was of no use; I couldn't sit or stand. I grabbed Roshi's kyosaku and seized her by the robe in desperation, but still I couldn't get it. Even when I was slapped on the cheek, poked with the kyosaku, and pushed away, *Mu* was out of my reach. I heard the voice of Roshi saying, "Around this time, Shakyamuni Buddha was struggling, covered in sweat. Think that your right hand is you, and your left hand is Shakyamuni Buddha, and do it!" *Ah, that's right! Shakyamuni Buddha was a human just like me.* As my body slowly became the body of the Buddha, I desperately prayed: *Namu Shakyamuni Tathagata, Namu Kanzeon Bodhisattva, Jizo Bodhisattva, Vairocana Buddha. All of the successive ancestors and teachers, please help me!*

Finally, the deadline I had given myself—3 p.m. on the seventh day—came and went, and then came the time for the last dokusan. The steel doors of my mind were not opening, no matter what I did. The rain started to fall outside. Roshi said, "Go out and practice while listening to the sound of the rain." I took an umbrella and went out into the darkness. My heart calmed down like still water. Sitting behind the building, I sunk into the sound of the rain. I don't know how much time passed, when suddenly my umbrella fell to the ground. In the instant I bent to pick it up—*Swoosh!*—suddenly all heaven and earth was penetrated. *Swoosh!*—this sound was filling the whole universe! *Kannon Bodhisattva, Jizo Bodhisattva, all the ancestors, my ordination teacher from my* hometown, my late mother—everyone is here, completely soaked in this rain. Swoosh!—everything is Mu! I broke through.

The last dokusan was at midnight. I went and was confirmed. Coming back from dokusan and trying again to sit, joy welled up in me. My laughter, about to overflow, could barely be contained.

At the end of sesshin, I went to the middle of a vegetable field and rolled around, laughing. Stretching out my hands and legs, I started to dance. My body was so light I could expand myself without limits. *Limitless, limitless.* I went to pay my respects to the statues of Jizo Bodhisattva and Vairocana Buddha, and they were smiling affectionately. Whatever I looked at was dear, beloved, intimate. Whatever I ate was delicious.

I wanted everyone in the world to taste this joy.

I know well that a lot of young nuns suffer, not knowing the purpose of human life. I realized that I have to continue to practice hard, really live from *Mu*, and save many people. This is my great mission. The Venerable Abbess says, "Just seeing the ox is not enough, you have to tame it well and control it with perfect ease. Never being tired of accumulating virtue is what we call Buddha. The Buddha Way is unsurpassable. Me too, I am still giving my all to remove defilements." How precious! Later I was told by my Dharma friends that during rohatsu sesshin, until the evening of the seventh day, not a single drop of rain fell. And again, soon after I had kensho, it all cleared out. Afterward, beautiful stars filled the sky, glittering and twinkling. The Venerable Abbess told me, "It was rain sent by the eight great dragon kings,[10] the good Dharma protectors came to save you." I have no words and can only shed tears of gratitude.

Gassho.

3

THE CROW OF A ROOSTER

Ms. Kazuko Kasashima

AT THE TIME when people were finally waking up from post-war lethargy, I began to contemplate the past and think about the future. As a result, I realized that what I had done for the last thirty precious years was just eat, sleep, wake up, laugh, cry, and get angry. I began in earnest to seek something more—an unshakable faith, no matter what circumstances might bring.

One day, my neighbor who had opened a private school for Western dressmaking told me that Sozen Nagasawa Roshi from the nun's training monastery was coming from Tokyo to give a lecture on *Shushogi*, and she highly recommended I attend. I agreed to go, but to be honest, I didn't care about the content of the lecture. I just thought, *I wonder what kind of person Roshi is?*

The moment I arrived, upon hearing the assembly of pure nuns chanting *Shushogi* with resounding voices, my tears started to flow spontaneously. In her lecture, Roshi said, "I am the universe! The universe is me!" And I exclaimed in my mind, *This is it! This is exactly what I have been seeking!*

In the past, I had tried three times to enter through the gate of Christianity, and each time I had returned with an empty heart. I had hunted for answers in self-help books. I had attended seminars about amateur drama theater, desperately trying to explore the reality of life and human nature. Still I was dissatisfied. Suddenly, after hearing this one talk, I felt like a weight in my chest had started to lift. Sadly, because of my work schedule, I was unable to attend the whole five days of lectures. But what I had gained by attending in part was an introduction to the practice of zazen and the certainty that it is possible to get out of this world of duality.

Eventually, not knowing anything of practice—not even knowing what the character for za in zazen was, I attended my first sesshin. Thanks to the heartfelt guidance I received for one week, I could wholeheartedly push myself with Mu, but the sesshin finished without me attaining real clarity. I vowed firmly in my heart to make as much effort as possible until the next sesshin in six months' time, and by any means necessary, to awaken.

After returning home, I drew the symbol of absolute oneness—a circle—in chalk all over a room that our family didn't use. Whenever possible, I would look at the room as a way to remind myself. Day and night, I would not let go of Mu or Jukku Kannon-gyo. I would prostrate to the Buddha in the morning and in the evening. I would chant sutras. On Sundays, although I am a late riser, I would get up at 5 a.m. and, after sitting one round of zazen, I would pay a visit to Soshin-an temple in Sekiya.

In the morning while it was still dark, in the evening when my family slept, and sometimes even during the day at a friend's house, I would sit zazen for thirty minutes or one hour at a time. I cast away being like an ordinary person, wanting to see this or hear that or wear this or that. Still, whenever I remembered about the trials and tribulations that buddhas and ancestors had endured in their practice, I knew that being lukewarm wouldn't be enough. A month before sesshin I got sick with a strong flu and, not to worry my family, I used it as an excuse to skip one meal a day as an offering, to strengthen my determination.

When the time for sesshin came, because my body was so weak, I wondered how I would even be able to leave the house. But then I got an injection that revived me, and until my departure, I was busy closing my business and private matters, preparing everything and leaving nothing undone. Walking through the streets I knew from childhood, I said my goodbyes: *Thank you for taking care of me for such a long time, Saha world. Goodbye! I am going to Nigorikawa to die.*[11] *But after I die, I will get reborn, become a beautiful person, and come back again!* Then I got on the bus. *This sesshin is the final sesshin of my life,* I resolved. With this great determination, I arrived and settled into my assigned sitting place.

However, unexpectedly, makyo started to appear one after another, attacking my eyes and ears. Different parts of my body— hands, legs, face, or sometimes the whole body—would shake incessantly. Some moments I felt pain and heat, as if I were being pierced with hot needles, and I thought that must be how death by electrocution feels. I tried to forget about the makyo, to get rid of it with *Mu,* to let go of it, but finally I came to the end of my resources and perseverance. *Why can't I practice smoothly like everybody else?* I wondered. *All the practice I did at home is crumbling here, together with the condition of my body. I came with such confidence, but maybe it was just conceit?* Bitter tears gushed out without stopping.

Despite the unceasing guidance and encouragement from Roshi and the support from Rev. Shudo, Ms. Nakayama, and the others, in this condition I was unable to make even small progress toward my goal. *My bad karma is very deep, and maybe that's why the Buddha, as a punishment, is not accepting my eager aspiration in this life,* I thought. *No matter what obstacle appears, I have to wake up from the dream of dualism and enter into the state of unity.* Remembering that this was my mission, I pulled myself together and went back to desperately practicing *Mu*.

I had decided that the third day would be the day I fulfilled my vow. So on the fourth day, when I found myself in the above state—a cowardly self, so pathetic and detestable—I was filled with the sense that even if I were to chop my body into pieces, it wouldn't be enough. Despite doing *Mu* with all my might, the tears of regret and disappointment flowed down my cheeks. I received words of admonition: "It is not the time for crying!" When I truly became miserable, even the tears wouldn't come out—only the tears of blood that were falling in my heart. *Is there something in this world comparable to this misery, this suffering, this regret?* I wondered. I ran to the Kannon-do, praying, *Shakyamuni Buddha! Kannon Bodhisattva! Ancestors! Have pity on me! Please, give me some power!* With my palms together, without thinking of what anyone would think about me, I cried in a loud voice, shedding tears of repentance.

On the fifth day, my body was getting weak, and together with it, *Mu* also seemed to weaken. The fact that I was skipping meals seemed to be the cause. I was cautioned by one of the nuns about it, and I decided I should eat three times a day from then on. During dokusan I received encouragement: "You have no energy. *Mu* is coming up in you already. You have to raise it up even more and go with this *MUUU!*" A new determination arose in me to practice with all my might. I knew that if I didn't obey those words, I would be so ashamed before Ni-Roshi that I wouldn't be able to go to dokusan at all.

After *kaichin* (formal end of the monastery's daily schedule), I went for night sitting. I tied a hand towel tightly around my head and wrapped myself in a blanket. Thinking of Bodhidharma, I closed my lips firmly, frowned my eyebrows, and opened my eyes wide. While listening to the voice of the frogs singing *Mu-*, *Mu-*, *Mu-*, I started to do *Mu-*, *Mu-*, *Mu-* in my belly. Yet again, a faint makyo started to appear, until the cold of the evening dew brought me back to my senses and to my practice.

On the sixth day, I calmly determined to think that there was no tomorrow. I decided that the time of fulfilling my vow would be the 3 p.m. dokusan that day. *Will it all be for nothing or will I become a buddha?* I wondered. With no exaggeration I saw that this moment was the final moment of truth. Until then, I had just kicked and squirmed without really throwing away my life. *For what and for whom did I come here?* I wondered. *Die! Die! Without dying, there is no getting the real thing! What is still holding me in this dream world of dualistic opposition? Isn't this the best possible place in the world to die? I will have a beautiful funeral service done for me! This time, whatever I hear, whatever I see, I won't let it distract me and I will sit with dignity,* I resolved.

The air in the hall was silent, and I was absorbed, inhaling with all my might, and then, without a sound, exhaling. After a while, as I had expected, my legs started to hurt as if they were jammed in a press. *Damn it! I won't give up! It is the last pain of this dying body. Let's savor it well!* I thought. My whole body was clammy from a cold sweat. My eyes wouldn't blink at all as I stared into the pillar. *There is no need to be caught up in anything. Only Mu-, Mu-, Mu-!* . . . Until what time was I in that state? When I became aware of it, the body that had been hurting all over felt completely light, without any sensations—and piercing the heavens, piercing through the earth, there was only *Mu*. This world that I had thought was so far away was close, only one step away. *Let's do it! Mu-, Mu-, Mu-!* Suddenly I heard the crow of a rooster—*cock-a-doodle-do!*—and in that instant, I broke through. *It is one! It is one! The universe is one! Just as Shakyamuni Buddha had said! I got it! I got it!* Spontaneously, deep laughter came out from the bottom of my belly.

Quickly, I should show this state to Roshi, I thought. I don't have any memory of how I ran to the Kannon-do. Roshi was standing there, and forgetting any etiquette, I leaped upon her. Full of tears of joy, I shouted, "I understood! I understood! The rooster crowed, and everything is *Mu!* Everything is *Mu!*" I looked at her face filled with a friendly, serene smile. I took her hands and turned her body in a circle.

The storm of deep emotion that blew through me is beyond all description. When I heard the resounding sound of the bell opening the 3 p.m. dokusan—*kan, kan, kan*—heaven and earth were one.

Gassho.

4

THE MOST WONDROUS PRINCIPLE

Rev. Kendo Kojima

SINCE THE ESTABLISHMENT of this country, until recently, Japan was never defeated in war. This was due to the widespread observance of Buddhist morality. Japan lost in World War II because the light of the Buddha had diminished, and our morality was sullied with dirt.

We had recently formed the Association of Nuns, and to fulfill our obligations as members of society, we nuns were sent to work in war plants. We organized groups that consoled evacuated children and tended to wounded soldiers, and we gave away a lot of our donations to the navy. As much as possible, we earnestly poured our energy into helping our country.

After the war, I turned my heart to the ideological front, fighting for equality for nuns in the Soto Zen tradition with the determination of a kamikaze. *All that the nuns of the past endured has been in preparation for this day,* I thought, and my resolve strengthened. Encouraged strongly by others, I became a director of the Association of Nuns. In a room on the second floor of the main office of the Soto school, I spread a banner saying: *Soto School's Nuns Association Headquarters.*

I set up my chair there on February 1, 1946. From the northern side, through a broken window, the cold wind blew continuously and mercilessly, but because of the passion running through my veins, I didn't feel it at all. At that time, we were starting to think about the prohibition on nuns giving Dharma transmission. We were waking up from past blindness and wanting to live as true nuns. Taking up this most important matter, together with Nagasawa Roshi, we embarked on a tour across the country. In every area we held a special general assembly of the Association of Nuns, and we held conferences stressing the extreme importance of nuns' Dharma transmission. We asked for signatures of support, and in March the same year, in a special meeting of the order, we called for the reform of our sect's constitution about Dharma transmission. Thus began our great fight to allow nuns to give shiho.

I was often in front of the order's commission, attending regular meetings of the order, or persistently petitioning with great effort in front of councils. Yet time after time we were mercilessly rejected. I cried to the heavens and prostrated to the earth, and I continued to shed bitter tears over the depth of the bad karma we had had for centuries. In the Dharma there is not supposed to be discrimination between man and woman. I tried to argue, "'Do not differentiate between men and women, this is a most wonderous principle of the Buddha Way'[12]—is this precious saying of our sect's founder merely empty words?" But it was in vain. In the end, I decided to stop arguing with them and to turn my gaze inward, to actually prove women can attain the Way. As the saying goes, "If you lay a strong foundation, even the roof will be sound." *Forget about being acknowledged or not,* I concluded. *Even if we are not acknowledged by a man-made system, reality—the Buddha-mind—will acknowledge us. If I throw myself completely into it and obtain and grasp the true form of the Dharma, then all will be well. Nuns are not outside the truth!* I threw myself into the practice community of the vice director of the Association of Nuns, Nagasawa Roshi, and her nuns' training monastery in Mitaka.

With such determination, I had no time for arguments about silent illumination Zen versus koan Zen. When seeing someone drowning in this very moment, there is no time to wonder from which side or what way to save them—just immediately act to save their life! Thus began my first fight on this Dharma battlefield, when I grappled with walking in the footprints of truth—during sesshin in February 1947.

I felt that if I could grasp this truth myself, I would also be able to resolve this most important matter of Dharma transmission for nuns, which weighed heavily on my shoulders. When I thought, *I have three thousand nuns on my back,* a mysterious and wonderful power would appear. It was life-and-death practice—raising all my courage and devoting all my passion. I entrusted myself completely, beseeching—*Namu Shakyamuni Buddha, namu Great Fearless Effort Buddha, have pity on me!* But even so, I was completely unable to realize the truth. *What is the way to Mu?* I wondered. However, knowing the time had arrived, I was determined to walk the way without stopping—even if I went at a snail's pace. *Mu-, Mu-, Mu-!—since I started practicing with Mu, how many months and years has it been that I have ceaselessly looked for the ox?*[13]

Then, before I knew it, I started to see the light of dawn. *Mu-, Mu-, Mu-!* ...

Roshi's kyosaku and strict words were becoming increasingly fierce—*Whack! Whack! Mu-, Mu-!* With my life on the line, I was overcome with a grim determination. At the last period of zazen—*Whack! Whack!*—*This is it!* I thought, and in that moment, I broke through. Great Universe—*Mu,* lively *Mu,* only

Kendo Kojima (chapter 4), second from the left; Shudo Sato (chapter 11),
third from the left; and other nuns and lay practitioners in the 1960s.

Mu, one-color *Mu*—life as well as death, all distinctions fell away. Only *Mu*! Finally I had broken through the first barrier. The tears of Dharma happiness and Zen joy streamed down. *Subject and object are one body*—for a moment the tears of great joy stopped, and I was smiling. *Will I ever see such beautiful scenery again? Truly, we are all children of truth*, I thought. Inside the Dharma of absolute oneness, when opening the Dharma eye, is there any discrimination between men and women? Dharma, just natural Dharma, completely revealed.

No matter how excellent a system we establish, if we don't investigate the source of Dharma, our order will be going straight down the path of degeneration. Looking at the world—with the development of chemistry and with the appearance of nuclear power—humanity has entered a dangerous period. But finally we are starting to wake up to the inherent love of peace. *Peace! World peace!* the voice of humankind is saying, without divisions between East and West. We must search for those ideals in Buddhism and master Zen. More and more people from America and Europe are starting to practice. We passionately campaign to spread the true Dharma of Mahayana Buddhism to the world. Yet in the midst of that enthusiasm, when I look at our country—the state of Japanese Buddhism gives me chills. Our established religious organizations are lethargic, and new religions are on the rise. Those very members of our order who don't have the Way-seeking mind and are not reflecting on themselves are the ones opposing us. Shouldn't they be sincerely concerned with the continuity of true Dharma transmission? We shouldn't still be differentiating between men and women. With renewed courage from attaining firm realization, I again stood up.

Right around the time we celebrated the seven-hundredth anniversary of our high ancestor's passing away, on April 1, 1952, a new amendment for our order was passed.[14] Finally we were granted the highest and most noble status of teachers: nuns were allowed to give Dharma transmission! Our long-cherished dream was achieved, and we were allowed entry into the vast gate of our founding ancestor's compassion. We became full members of our sect, following the Four Great Vows while coming and going in life and death. How truly sacred. How extremely precious. With self-respect and self-love, we should carry out our mission as Zen nuns—being intimate with sitting; practicing Zen; falling seven times, getting up eight times; praying for friendship between ourselves; and practicing and progressing on this one-way path. By the merit of sitting, we benefit the world and save people—this is the most wondrous principle.

Gassho.

5

GREAT CRY OF A NEWBORN

Rev. Ryojun Nakano

IT IS EMBARRASSING to say, but when I was first at the monastery and heard phrases like "delusional thinking," it was hard for me—a naive person—to believe that all human thinking is delusion. At times, even an antipathy would arise in me and I would think, *Ah this monastery, it stinks with sanctimony.* I felt that if that was my attitude, there was no point in training there, but still I was unable to suppress what was arising in me. Sometimes I would burst into a fit of anger inside, but outwardly I would just silently sit, filled with loneliness and dissatisfaction. Night after night I would jump out of bed and study *Shobogenzo*, seeking an answer.

I had entered the monastery in the fall, and before rohatsu I was able to do three sesshins. I clearly told Roshi, "I believe in having kensho and becoming a buddha," but hearing myself say the word *kensho* made me feel pretentious.

During the rohatsu sesshin, I worked for three days in the kitchen. The first morning, when standing before the altar for the Dharma protector Idasonten, a line suddenly came to my mind: "In the middle of practice, seeing life and death." *That's right, it is now!* I thought, and my attitude shifted. As I pressed the pump beside the well, calmly filling the bucket with water, I would chant *Mu-, Mu-, Mu-!* When polishing a pot, I would polish it with all my might, even if it was already shining. Yet when I heard the sound of kyosaku from the zendo, it bothered me, and I couldn't concentrate. I burned the rice and overcooked the soup every day.

After my three days of kitchen duty passed, I vowed that I would really put my life on the line. As we sat in meditation, people on both sitting platforms were getting beaten—*Whack! Whack!*—but I was not getting the kyosaku at all, which made me angry. During the last sesshin, I asked in dokusan, "Please give the kyosaku to me as well." The words with which the Venerable Abbess adamantly refused have stayed in my ears since then: "You are not entitled yet to receive the kyosaku of buddhas and ancestors. You are still a baby." *I am a human being! I came here because I want to awaken!* I thought. *Alright then, Mu-, Mu-, Mu-! Until the final victory, Mu-, Mu-, Mu-! Cut off any pride and doubt! Where is discrimination, where is consciousness? Cut it off! Mu-, Mu-, Mu-! Kill it!*

On the evening of day four, I glimpsed the timeless self. Hearing the bell, I ran to dokusan. Roshi gave me a few kind words. Then my practice slackened, and again my arrogance came out. I found myself smirking at those who were dozing off. *The arrogance just changes form,* I realized. *I should quickly cut it out! Mu-, Mu-! Die! Mu-, Mu-, Mu-!*

On day five, maybe because I was trying too hard and practicing too forcefully, my head was spacey and I was unable to practice at all. I was unsteady and dejected.

Day six was quite intense. I put a razor under my sitting mat, resolving that if the smirking one wouldn't die, I would stab her to death. Out of nowhere, I got hit with the kyosaku. *Will I let them hit me with the kyosaku?* I turned to the side. *I want to quickly leave the human realm. I cannot stand sitting on this mat. I don't want to live even one second more.* I took the razor in my hand, but there was something in me that didn't want to die. *This is so difficult! What is making me suffer so much? I must quickly save myself!*

Zazen ended, and I took my sitting mat into the corridor. At that time a makyo appeared, and everything before my eyes was filled with flowers, and I prayed: *Shakyamuni Buddha, have mercy. Great teacher-ancestors, have pity. Please guide me into the bright world. Please quickly help this suffering one.* Before I knew it, I was sitting inside a storeroom, but I couldn't stand it there either. I went to the Venerable Abbess and asked her if I could sit in the barn outside. "You mustn't break the rules of this monastery. Just sit on the mat at your place," she refused firmly.

I couldn't go on just staring uselessly at the wooden wall. *If I cannot live in clarity, I should kill myself. I should leave this place, it is so painful.* Again I heard the Venerable Abbess's voice urging us to attain kensho. I fell further into irritation. *What is that? Are we kensho beggars? How filthy!* I was completely fed up with this practice place full of beggars for kensho. *Okay, I should leave here, go to the mountain at the back, and read the* Shobogenzo *of our school's founder. I still cannot die. There is something deep inside that doesn't want to die.*

A bell for the end of zazen rang. As I got up for kinhin, I staggered, and in that instant: *This is the world of Mu! This is the world of Mu!* I have no memory of that kinhin. When I became aware again, I was in the toilet, shouting, "The world of *Mu!* Ha!" It was so easy—so vast, vast, vast. I also don't remember how I went back to kinhin. Then when a person on the sitting platform to my left was getting kyosaku, the monitor said, "This is it!" And when my ear heard *Whack!!*—in that instant—I broke through.

Ha, ha, ha! The bottom of it all fell away, my whole body became light, and I was unable to say anything. *Am I still on earth?* I wondered. A forceful trembling wouldn't stop. At that moment, for the first time, I wanted to go to the dokusan room and shout as if to destroy everything. Later I heard from the others that I was crying loudly.

Namu Bodhisattva of Great Love, Great Compassion Kannon! "The one who is bowing and the one who is bowed to, both of serene empty nature"[15]—those words and their spirit of mutual support gushed forth from the bottom of my heart like a cry of a newborn. For the first time, a sense of gratitude welled up for my dear, caring teachers. I turned in the direction of my hometown and was filled with deep appreciation for all the people who taught me.

People on the sitting platform were groaning, *Mu-, Mu-, Mu-!* I prayed that they might quickly enter into this bright world. The sound of cars—*brrrrrrr*—full of energy; the sound of the bell calling for chanting—*kan, kan*—a lively world that is myself. *Gong*—the sound of the *keisu* (bowl-shaped gong) during evening chanting pierced my whole body. *We are on holy Vulture Peak with Shakyamuni Buddha himself! I will dedicate the merit from this chanting to the multitudes of beings,* I thought. "*Namu kara tanno . . .*"[16]—each line flew from my mouth. That evening I went to bed, but I was not able to sleep a wink.

Tomorrow again I will go to the kitchen and will give my all for the Dharma warriors fighting *Mu-, Mu-, Mu-!*

Gassho.

6

BASKING IN THE WINTER MOON

Ms. Harue Hiroe

MY FAMILY BELONGED to the parish of Higashi Hongan-ji temple. I was raised very strictly—my parents were passionately religious people, and we gathered at our home to chant sutras in the morning and the evening. From a young age I developed a mind of faith. However, just relying on the external power of original vow felt somehow not enough,[17] so I read many different Buddhist texts and magazines. Even after I married and we moved to the countryside for my husband's work, the most important thing to me was to always visit temples, no matter which school of Buddhism they belonged to.

Around ten years ago we moved to the town of Chofu in Tokyo prefecture. I learned from a person in the neighborhood that every month a group of nuns came to the area for takuhatsu. I had an unusually strong feeling about these nuns and secretly awaited their arrival. One day, from the entrance of the house, I heard the sound of chanting and bells. I ran outside and saw a few young nuns who, despite this world's concern with glamor, were walking in black robes without any decorations, in *waraji* (rice straw sandals) and *kyahan* (gaiters), with hats made of bamboo worn low on their heads. Seeing them chanting sutras so bravely and nobly, I was overwhelmed with intense emotion and moved to tears. I gave them alms, but when they left, I felt somehow dissatisfied. I looked forward to seeing them again.

The next time they came, I asked them to chant sutras at our modest home altar, and I prepared coffee for them on the porch in the inner garden as an offering. After a joyful conversation, I inquired about which temple they were from and whether I could meet with their Venerable Abbess.

As soon as it was possible, my husband and I paid a visit to Kannon-ji. We asked the Abbess to come once a month to give a Dharma talk and perform a ceremony for our ancestors at our home. She said, "If it was just about chanting sutras, then there are many other temples and someone else could do it. But if you want a Dharma talk, I will come."

From then on, every month we were able to hear the Abbess's *teisho* (formal Dharma talk) and receive her guidance. I learned for the first time that I had been lost in the dream of my delusion, believing Buddha to be something other than me. The more deeply I listened, the more I understood that Buddha is all the phenomena of this vast, limitless universe—there is nothing that is not Buddha. I was told that I am also a part of it and that the Buddha was the one who had fully awakened to this truth, completely embodied it, and become a great guiding teacher.

I was shocked by this marvelous Dharma, deeply impressed, and ashamed of my ignorance. Hearing that it is impossible to know this state of mind without going beyond the perception of the six senses and realizing it for oneself, I knew I had to gather my courage, overcome my fears, and enter into practice. I arranged to attend a sesshin.

The Venerable Abbess sat in the center of the zendo at Kannon-ji. Lines of nuns and laywomen—young and old—sat motionless on either side of her, their noble postures like stone or wooden Buddha statues. To one side I saw a blackboard with the words "Wake up to your true nature." *Ah, this is it!* I thought, and I felt a deep regret that I hadn't known about it until now, even though I was sixty-five years old. This was a merciless world—I might not wake up tomorrow, and yet I had not practiced. I felt ashamed of myself, but I summoned the determination that no matter what, I would do it. Filled with courage, I went to my seat.

During lunch we ate in a very solemn and orderly way. Thanks to the chants we did before and after meals, I realized how unconsciously I had been eating. Food is a blessing, and I felt deep gratitude. Seeing the formal way of drinking tea each day during sesshin, I realized where the practice of tea ceremony I enjoyed so much had come from. I thought about all the young girls out there and how valuable it would be for them to attend such ceremonies as well as zazen practice itself.

Soon I received the koan *Mu* like everybody else. Since I lived in the neighborhood, I was staying at home and commuting to the temple daily. At first my mind was scattered, and I couldn't practice in earnest. But with the passing days—thanks to the morning teisho, where we received guidance from the Venerable Abbess, and encouragement with the stick—little by little I was able to get my mind under control.

Every morning and evening I walked through the open plains of Mitaka, past vegetable fields and through forests. When I saw the vegetables shining with morning dew, each of them obediently fulfilling their mission, racing to grow quickly, my palms would come together in gassho, and I was embarrassed for us humans, for how shameful we are. I could hear the rustle of fallen leaves under foot, and I had the feeling that these leaves were also fulfilling their mission. Seeing the moon shining brightly in the great sky, sometimes I would turn to it and practice *Mu-, Mu-, Mu-!*, standing absorbed for thirty or forty minutes.

During zazen I was attacked by various makyo that would appear on the shoji in front of me—a horse's face, a cow's face, the Buddha, or figures of monks. When I received the kyosaku, I would straighten out. Gradually, though, with the passing of time, I wanted to sit more and more, and when the bell for kinhin rang, I would be disappointed. One time I thought I had gotten it and went for dokusan, but I was told firmly, "No good." Another time the tears of pure repentance flowed down my face without stopping. The Venerable Abbess said, "Throw yourself away! Throw yourself away!" When I was young, my art teacher had said the same thing. *So that's what he meant,* I thought. I forgot about my surroundings and became completely absorbed, intensely doing *Mu-, Mu-, Mu-!*, sweat pouring down my body.

On the seventh day, in the afternoon, a nun stood at my back from the beginning to the end of sitting, to encourage me. I felt as if she was pushing me from behind. During dokusan I was utterly absorbed, unaware of my surroundings. In the zendo I kept sitting, unaware of kinhin. I was practicing with all my might, putting my life on the line, when suddenly—*Ahhh!* The cold and pure wind touched me, and in that instant, I broke through. My whole body started to violently shake, and the dark clouds that were until now gathered above my head were instantly blown away.

I broke through to the fresh, impossible-to-express world of *Mu.* I was overwhelmed with gratitude. Even if I had tried to say how happy I was to have made all that effort, I wouldn't have been able to say a word. I went to dokusan, embraced the teacher, and cried. For a while I couldn't stop the tears, thanking the Kannon Bodhisattva standing in the zendo, Monju Bodhisattva, and various buddhas until I calmed down. Later I was able to find the words to express my gratitude to the nuns for their encouragement.

Sesshin ended and I had a small confirmation ceremony before leaving with a houseman who had come to pick me up. Late that night, turning into December 8, mist filled the whole world. Without thinking, I said to the houseman, "It is here, it is here." But he was confused, asking, "What is it? What do you mean, Madame? I don't understand." Remembering Shakyamuni Buddha's great kensho from thousands of years before, I felt full of gratitude. *How blessed I am,* I thought. I had received deep guidance from both my teacher and Shakyamuni Buddha.

There is no way I can convey my gratitude for being able to reach such a blessed state of mind at this noble rohatsu sesshin. I am so grateful to the teacher who foreswore sleep and food so she could guide us, and to the nuns for their encouragement. I am only able to repay my gratitude by inviting as many people as possible to walk this path. This has become my mission.

Gassho.

7

SHARING THE JOY
OF AWAKENING

Rev. Kanko Ishimoto

HAVING RECEIVED THIS difficult-to-receive human body, and having met with the hard-to-meet true Dharma, I am truly grateful. I can't help but prostrate before a thousand buddhas and a million ancestors, shedding tears of joy.

After the war, the state of our society worsened. People were only concerned with living, finding food, and making their reputations. They were becoming slaves to money, depraved. It was truly a pitiful sight, so many lost people without faith. Every day the newspaper reported on the increase in crime. Everywhere you looked, the world was full of falsehood. *Are things really okay like that? Where is the truth?* People's conversations lacked warmth and authenticity. *Why do human beings exist at all?* I had not the slightest idea. I longed to hear about something of the highest importance. *Any doctrine is fine,* I thought. I just wanted to listen to a true teaching, to rely on someone dignified who could give me peace of mind.

Everything around me seemed to condemn me—when the dog barked or if a cat meowed. Even the plants seemed to say, *Why are you not practicing? How can you be so irresponsible?* Each time I saw a young person looking like a yakuza, I felt that we monastics were not doing enough to help cultivate all beings, and if we continued like this, Japan would simply fall into ruin. The future looked dark, and those who should save people were the people of religion. I thought, *I should do real training, chant true sutras, and go for real takuhatsu—then I would know what to do about the crisis in our country and what we could say so that the youth could help us rebuild it.*

As the days went by, this aspiration deepened, especially as I saw more people dying. I couldn't bear this life of grasping at clouds, without any real clarity, and I didn't want to be one of the many dying without any faith and without being prepared. *How in the world can one grasp the absolute truth?* I wondered. For my own peace of mind and liberation, and for the peace and welfare of all humankind, I felt that by all means I had to resolve this great problem. I started to wonder if the key to resolving this great problem was zazen.

Even in this Dharma-ending age, I deeply believed that the true Dharma was not yet extinguished. When I finally had an opportunity to visit a true teacher, I was so grateful for that good karma that I cried with joy. *This is what I have been looking for.* I resolved that no matter how hard it would be, I absolutely had to destroy this long-standing castle of defilements and delusions—my own and everyone's.

However, no matter how hard things are in the world, there is nothing harder than zazen. If you cannot take on the suffering of the Great Universe, you will not attain the happiness of the Great Universe either. To attain the joy of this timeless indestructibility, this great peace of mind, one has to see through every obstacle and put all of one's life into this one breath.

At first my legs were in pain; just sitting in a lotus posture was difficult. Becoming one with pain, fighting with the body, fighting with the mind—it was a bloody, desperate struggle. "If one dies the Great Death, one will be the most alive," said the teacher. Hearing those kind, encouraging words, my body started to shake. I was determined to see through *Mu* with this very breath. Yet the more earnest I was, the more delusional thoughts appeared. For the first time, I realized how ugly and shameful my mind was. The more one does zazen, the more this becomes clear, I realized. *If I don't jump into it with total honesty, I won't be able to meet with true Buddha.*

All the buddhas of the three worlds, all successive generations of ancestors, went through the most difficult experiences in their training for the sake of the Way. They believed that they, too, were one of the buddhas. That belief generated in them a fierce determination, like a red-hot iron ball piercing into the world of *Mu*. Transcending body and mind is even more difficult than a painful death. Dokusan was do or die. Again, I thought, *If I don't penetrate the realm of absolute oneness, if I don't realize it, I will never be able to escape from the cycle of birth and death and delusion. Aren't both buddhas and sentient beings endowed with the unborn and indestructible Buddha-nature?* I continued to practice, vowing that even if I were to die, I would not get up from my seat. I would just practice—purely, endlessly, meticulously.

On the morning of the third day of sesshin, I became a ball of flames. I single-mindedly stared into *Mu*. On the paper screen before me, the upper part of Kannon Bodhisattva's body appeared, emanating light. Spontaneously I started to pray. But soon after this joy, I came back to myself, thinking, *Ah, this is makyo*. I continued my practice as if to destroy it; I would not allow even a small gap of carelessness. "If you think you can do it, without fail you will. Rely on Buddha, rely completely. It is no time for crying"—the strict words of the Venerable Abbess pierced through my flesh and bones. Casting off everything, I prostrated myself to the great earth and relied entirely on Buddha.

The faith that gushes forth from the depths within us—that is the real faith. All the buddhas of the three worlds are sitting with us, trying to help us. How truly grateful I was, how precious this zendo was, filled with earnestness, intensity, a life-and-death struggle. *One ten-thousand-mile-long iron bar . . .*,[18] with strong faith I pushed forward. The Venerable Abbess continued to press me, saying with her frightening face, "Show me *Mu!* Come on, show it!" I had run out of tears, and my voice wouldn't come out anymore. It was a pain and anguish not of this world.

When I had almost reached the point of screaming "I can't do it anymore!" strangely, a new strength rose up in me. Going beyond the anguish of body and mind, I was able to make progress. Slowly I gained the confidence that I could do it.

Only Mu is completely doing Mu. There is no enlightenment or lack of enlightenment, just Mu. There is no delusion, or lack of delusion, only Mu. Even if I were not to eat for ten days, I wouldn't fall over if I go forward with this spirit. I can do it in twenty minutes, I can do it in ten minutes, one minute, even one second . . . I heard a voice behind me, "That's it!" I don't know if it was the encouragement of the Venerable Abbess or of the buddhas and ancestors, but it felt as if fire was blasting out of my eyes and blood was coming out of every pore of my body. *This has to be the absolute worst anguish,* I thought.

Then, all at once, truly, I glimpsed the world of *Mu.* The ticking of the clock, the sound of the kyosaku, the sound of the bell— everything was *Mu,* together with me. *Monju Bodhisattva is Mu, the Venerable Abbess is Mu, I am Mu, everyone in the zendo is Mu— everything I can see, everything I can hear—there is absolutely nothing that is not Mu.* Filled with confidence, I went to dokusan. "The skin of the balloon is not yet broken—it is just a transparent skin. But if you pierce it even a little bit, it will break." The Venerable Abbess could see that if there is even a hair-width gap or a falsehood the size of a feather, one cannot attain the highest and most noble treasure. With an honest and pure heart, I plunged forward, and in that instant—*It is Mu!* The balloon of duality burst. *The universe is one. Heaven and earth—same root, all myriad things—one body.*[19] I broke through. *Such joy!* I almost fainted. *Below and above the heavens, I alone am the World-Honored One!*[20]

I was not at all concerned with how I looked in front of the others. I tried to stand and sit, shake and clap my hands—no matter what I did, it was reality. I didn't know what to do with myself from the joy, and I did a little dance. I was like a baby Tathagata. *This joy is thanks to all the troubles the Venerable Abbess took for me until now. She is truly a kind and beloved mother of great love and great compassion,* I thought.

Last spring I had lied that I was going out for a long takuhatsu, and instead I went to the nunnery to participate in this sesshin. Thanks to that, my old ordination teacher and I attained buddhahood together. It was tough; it was truly tough. This body-mind, filled with delusive obscurations, had to sweat. It had to purify through tears and come to the verge of death to liberate itself and grasp this world, this indestructible and timeless realm, this life, this joy. "Zazen is rightly the Dharma gate of joyful ease"[21]—it is boundlessly wide and deep. If I stretch out my hands, they reach to the end of the world. How exhilarating it is to wake up from the dream of complete darkness and suddenly fly out into a bright and expansive world, so bright it dazzles. *So those are my hands?* I wondered, and I don't know how many times I rubbed and touched them. *So this is tatami? This is* koromo (a long sleeved robe)? *This is the sound of the bell? This is the ticking of the clock?* It resounded so far; it resounded through the whole universe.

When our being returns to a state of absolute unity, we see and hear everything as if for the first time. Everything is interesting and new. I understood that, until now, I had just been watching a dream of deep, deep delusion—how embarrassing! I repented from the bottom of my heart and laid down this burden I had carried through lifetimes and worlds. Both my body and mind were light and at ease. *Right here is the highest Pure Land.* Whether I was wiping something with a rag or holding a broom, my body was light and fresh. I was invigorated and felt free as I went about my activities. Every move of a hand, every step taken, was entirely the Buddha's deeds and the Buddha's actions. When chanting the sutras, I truly chanted the sutras. When listening to teisho, I was finally able to nod my head in agreement. Even the plants seemed to be singing praise to this immense virtue, and being in nature, I was in high spirits. When I prostrated in deep gratitude, the buddhas and ancestors also prostrated with me. *Isn't the blood of Shakyamuni Buddha and all ancestors ceaselessly flowing in my body? It is now that I have become a true disciple of Buddha,* I thought, as more tears flowed down my cheeks.

I want all people of the world to grasp this true joy. My mission is to lead others into this realm of Buddha. The more I receive it with gratitude, the heavier the responsibility becomes. The fact that I have received this difficult-to-receive human body and, moreover, met this difficult-to-meet true Dharma is entirely thanks to the providence of the buddhas and ancestors, and to the Venerable Abbess. I am full of inexhaustible gratitude. To somehow repay this great blessing, my real practice starts now. To fulfill this great vow through lifetimes and worlds, I will continue right mindfulness. Each time I reach the top of the mountain, there is another mountain, another profound koan. Each small action, life after life, world after world, is a practice given by the universe, a practice of great peace and ease.

Three worlds are mind alone; both peace and war are born of the human mind. We must make our mind beautiful, just, and peaceful, basing it on the Buddha's teachings. We must find there our peace and liberation and contribute to the peace and welfare of all humanity. In the end, I believe that this is the most important matter for the Soto school. This one true Way cleanses society of its ills and elevates the world to buddhahood. I believe that there is no other path than that. I can only single-mindedly prostrate myself, with my hands in gassho.

8

BECOMING A PEACEFUL PERSON

Ms. Aiko Nakano

I AM A TWENTY-TWO-YEAR-OLD girl. Ever since I remember, I have been reading sutras and listening to conversations about zazen. As I was the youngest child, I was spoiled. When I became sulky, I wouldn't listen to anybody—I was so stubborn. Even when I started going to school, I was very selfish. Unless I was getting special treatment, I wouldn't obey.

I was twelve when my mother—who had been in bed with a long-term illness—passed away. From then on, my father made desperate efforts to turn me into an elegant and obedient child, but I only envied the kids who had mothers. I became a very dark and rebellious girl, looking only for other peoples' faults. Although at school my grades were good, and I wanted to believe that all the teachers were trying to teach me how to be a person of virtue, I didn't respect them. I was unable to bow my head, even in front of my father, who himself had had kensho. There was no one I could look up to.

One day, my father told me the Venerable Abbess from the nuns' training monastery in Mitaka would be coming to visit us, so I should return home early from school. This was the first time I met the Abbess, and meeting her felt as if I were meeting the Buddha himself. Over time, gradually she became like a mother to me.

Whenever I felt lonely, I would search through my father's books and read all the articles by the Abbess and other nuns, as well as all the easily understandable Zen texts I could lay my hands on. What precious teachings they were! Yet people around me seemed to be just playing around as if they didn't have a worry in the world, completely unconcerned. This seemed to me so strange.

Although I was able to understand Zen theory, I sensed there was something elusive not captured by the words. When I heard the Venerable Abbess talk, I was aware of that mystery underneath what was spoken. From the depths of my heart, I wanted to be able to comprehend the Abbess's talks and letters. The Abbess said, "You will truly start to understand my talks after awakening," and I knew she was right. I needed the same Dharma eye as her. Slowly I started to feel drawn to do zazen.

During that time, maybe because I was struggling so much, my body was weak, and I couldn't sit still for even two minutes. But I did just as I was instructed—rested and rested—and meanwhile I pressed Jizo stamps,[22] copied sutras, and recited *Jukku Kannon-gyo*. I was praying to be able to participate in sesshin. The Abbess had told me to come, even if only for one day. I constantly thought about the weakness of my body, my many duties at home, and how I could get a few days off work. I decided that no matter how hard it would be, I would go.

My first sesshin was in April 1951. I was worried that I would be an obstacle for everyone and inconvenience them with my sickness, but I was able to complete the week without any problems. After that, I attended sesshins of three or five days, or even just one night—whatever my circumstances would allow. I was told that daily practice was important, so I was also sitting at home as much as possible. And without missing a single day, I was pressing Jizo stamps. I was close to completing two hundred thousand of them.

My stepmother would sometimes say, "Why don't you dress nicely and go see a movie?" But even when I tried to put makeup on, I didn't want to see my face like that. Unless beauty comes from my mind, it is useless. When I would reluctantly go to see a movie, even if it was fun in the moment, later I would unbearably suffer.

Gradually I got healthy. My parents told me I should work as a sewing teacher. But how could I stand in front of people and teach them when I felt so inferior? I vowed that by any means, I would have kensho.

Finally I went to the March sesshin, leaving my very sick father behind. I threw myself into it, ready to die. Fearing that my father would die before my awakening, I practiced as if possessed. Although I was motivated by these painful thoughts, for some reason I didn't succeed. "You don't have to force yourself. There will surely come a time when you will get it," the Abbess and my father said to me. Although I cried and cried, I tried to heed their teaching.

The Abbess and my parents cared for me more than anyone else in this world. I thought if only I said "Yes!" with all my life, if only I followed their guidance, surely it would go well. I felt as if I had boarded a great ship. As instructed by the Abbess, I bowed to Jizo Bodhisattva, to Kannon Bodhisattva, to my parents. I tried to be an obedient and kind daughter, and morning and night I prayed I would awaken. Despite this, I was not able to change my argumentative nature, and sometimes I would explode and say frightening things. To oppose my father I said, "I won't be going

After rohatsu sesshin in 1951. Ms. Aiko Nakano in front row, second from left.

to visit the Abbess anymore, and I won't practice zazen in this life ever again!" But my father acted as if nothing had happened, and he took me on the Saigoku pilgrimage of thirty-three temples.[23]

During the pilgrimage, I was standing in front of a Kannon statue and tears welled up. I felt sorry, thinking, *I must become a good daughter. Venerable Abbess, I am sorry.* I cried in gassho with all my heart. I felt this change of heart was the grace of Kannon Bodhisattva. From there I went straight to the nuns' training monastery for a *wago-kai*,[24] and in dokusan the Abbess said kindly, "You have become warmer, so come for sesshin, even one day is fine." I felt I had my life back.

At the next sesshin I attended, the Abbess said, "If you are determined to follow your father who had kensho—whether to hell or to the Pure Land—then certainly you will have kensho yourself. I bet my life on it." She stared into my eyes as she said these words. I felt so sorry. "No matter how much I repent, my karma doesn't become any lighter," I said, and the Venerable Abbess replied, "Before having kensho, everybody is like that. When you awaken, it is the first true step of repentance."

From then on, I just served my parents as much as I could, and my argumentativeness didn't appear at all. It came to the point that even my stepmother said she wanted to somehow repay me for my kindness. It was wonderful. I was waiting for my father's concern for me to lessen, and I finally received permission to participate in the next sesshin.

Arriving in the afternoon, I could hear the familiar sound of people voicing *Mu* out loud. I was told not to do so myself, so I just continued to sit silently, settling my breath, and it became indescribably quiet. The Abbess told me, "If you don't have complete trust that you can do it, you will get unsteady. Finish it off in the next two days!" Although I was practicing hard, I was unable to do it.

In dokusan on the morning of the sixth day, I complained that my legs hurt and I was in pain, and was told, "Don't strain yourself. A twenty-ounce box becomes full with twenty ounces. If you try to practice in the same manner as others, it is inappropriate."

One of the nuns, Rev. Shudo, advised me, "Exhale deeply, settle in your belly, and then inhale. During the exhale you become *Mu*," and she kindly practiced it with me. However, my breath would not settle, and I felt anxiety in my chest to the point where my breath would stop. And since I was thinking too much, I kept forgetting how to work with *Mu*. I went to dokusan asking to be taught again. Gradually I started to be able to breathe into my lower belly without any pain.

On the morning of the seventh day, I was told to see *Mu* and hear *Mu*. Following that, doing kinhin, suddenly I heard the sound of something banging on the roof. I looked up and saw that the roof was wet. I was happy—I love rain, so I felt renewed resolve. During teisho we were told, "There is nothing better than rain falling on the last day of sesshin. In the past, many people who did *Mu* together with the rain had kensho. Actually, everybody wants to awaken, but Mara is more comfortable, so they just entertain themselves with trivial things. They don't follow, no matter how much they are pulled. If you really understood how much trouble you cause to others, you would certainly do it." From the bottom of my belly the words *I am sorry!* welled up. Without looking away, I began to stare into *Mu*, together with the rain. The sound of the bell sounded with *Mu-, Mu-, Mu-!* The ticking of the clock sounded a calm *Mu-, Mu-, Mu-!* I went to dokusan and was told, "You are gradually getting closer. Don't get careless!" Then I started to see *Mu*. I went for dokusan again but was told, "As long as you don't become one and suddenly break through— that's still not it!" During the next round, I spaced out. When I went into dokusan again, the Venerable Abbess said, "Before you said you started to see *Mu*, but now you are not sure if it's false or true. Bring to dokusan a firmer *Mu!*" "Yes!" I said, and started to bow, and both the Abbess and the bell became *Mu*, and gradually everything started to become *Mu*. Even the shadows when everyone moved were *Mu*—yet I knew the dokusan was soon coming to an end, and I needed a firmer *Mu*.

"Until a splendid *Mu* comes, even if the dawn comes, don't get up!" said the Abbess in the next dokusan, staring intensely at me. *Mu-*, *Mu-*, *Mu-!* As she hit me on my knee, in that instant— there it was! I broke through and grabbed the Abbess, crying and laughing. "Not yet, not yet. If you laugh too much, your energy will get wild and you won't be able to respond to my questions," she told me, and she sent me back to sit again. But no matter what she asked after that, I was able to reply. I became childlike and strange, and the laughter just overflowed. I felt sorry for the nuns who were doing their practice with all their hearts, so I hid my face as I was laughing.

At the 6 p.m. dokusan, I received the next koan. I had passed *Mu*. The Venerable Abbess said solemnly, "To repay your gratitude to me, the only thing to do is to become a good daughter to your mother." I realized that Kannon Bodhisattva—the one who came to save me, the one to whom I owe gratitude—was my true stepmother. I vowed, "I will become a good daughter!" In the same way the Venerable Abbess saved me, I felt love for all people and wanted to save them.

At the end of the retreat someone said, "When you came here, you were crying and thinking of dying, but finally you have made it!" Now I feel like I didn't suffer at all. To be confirmed, to have what I had been longing for day and night—to awaken—was worth everything. The nuns were happy for me, saying, "Your father will be delighted!" My deceased mother and older brother, who attained buddhahood together, must be filled with relief.

The Venerable Abbess told me, "Don't be wary of people. Become a person who can take anyone into her heart. This is what it means to be a peaceful person." I truly aspire to be that way. Venerable Abbess, and everyone, thank you so much for taking care of me for so long. How much effort you have put into that!

Gassho.

9

THE SWEET FRUIT OF PRACTICE

Rev. Zuiho Arakawa

WHAT SHOULD I WRITE? How can I write about it? Heaven and earth move of their own accord, and I feel like I should restrain myself from writing a foolish human description of it. How deeply sad it is that humans live by the small notions that we impose on ourselves! We sink into sorrow, flare up in criticism, shake with anger—these are the feelings that generated such desperation in me that, in 1955, I went for sesshin.

At my first dokusan, Roshi, sitting straight and looking at me with her piercing eyes, said, "Don't end up with the head of a dragon but the tail of a snake!" *I will do it. I want to do it. I have to do it.* Holding this determination like a fireball, I left her.

From night until morning, I chased *Mu*, but each time I went to dokusan, the *Mu* I thought I had grasped crumbled without leaving any trace, leaving me only with bitter tears. On top of the tears, the sweat poured down; on top of the sweat, tears flowed. Roshi said, "I am sure you realize how much people before you suffered to see *Mu*."

Two days passed. Three days passed. Impermanence is swift, like a strong wind. The sweat and tears started to dry, and before I knew it, I was heading into the middle of sesshin with intense judgment and opposition growing in my mind.

My right shoulder started to hurt from the kyosaku I received day after day. I developed a blister, and then it broke. The more desperate my practice grew, the more extreme the fierceness of the kyosaku became. No matter how strong my determination was, no matter how much effort I gave to it, I was unable to bear the physical pain. I knew I should consider the kyosaku precious, but I resented it. I was afraid of it and pitied myself for trembling in fear. Then I grew angry, and I was not able to stop rebelling against it, thinking, *I will absolutely not awaken after being beaten! I will do it with my own strength. I will do it with the power of my own practice. What's the worth of awakening after being hit by someone?* These thoughts consumed my mind, leaving me unable to gratefully accept the precious kyosaku.

However, the Buddha-mind was not paying any attention to that. If I were careless even for a moment, immediately the stick would fly to my right shoulder and burn like fire. It was painful and difficult. *Why do I have to be beaten from morning to night? Give me a break and leave me alone!* I thought. I burned with this one aim of having kensho, but I wanted to do it with my own power, my own strength. My ego was all worked up. *I didn't even come here for kensho, nor did I plan to sit here to be beaten up. Please give me a break! Ah, it is so tough. I am unable to continue in this anguish indefinitely . . . What will come out of practicing while suffering so much? The tiredness and suffering penetrating this body and mind, this idiot Zuiho, being whacked for the whole week. Bleeding from my shoulder, ruining my throat—I cannot live like this. If I want to escape from here, I should do it as fast as possible. Right now, right now!* On the one hand, I was doing *Mu* and receiving the precious kyosaku. On the other hand, I was making this kind of decision to leave.

I should run away after the next lunch. The best way would be to go from Shinagawa station to Karasuyama. I can't go to Sengawa because there is the danger of being found. How should I prepare? Does it matter? As long as I have money, I can go and find my way. Where will I go? I should go to my friend's place, to Higashimatsuhara. Mu-, Mu-, Mu-! If I am to run away soon, why am I making such effort to practice? It's not very like me. What am I afraid of? I wanted to rest a little bit, and without any sound, I wiped my sweat away. Then I heard a voice above my head: "If you want to awaken, don't spare even one instant. What are you doing wiping your sweat away as if you have time to spare?"—*Whack! Whack!*

Ah, shut up, shut up! Okay, I have decided to run away today no matter what. I cannot take any more of this old monastery from a century ago! But if I were to run away, I would have to change clothes. So I guess I have to leave at night. Maybe it would be better to go after kaichin and head toward Sengawa. I will pretend I am going for yaza (informal night-sitting) . . . *But it is still so far to the end of the day! The only thing I can think of is now—so at least I should get rid of this judgmental mind that I have because of my deep bad karma. Until my breath stops, I should practice. No matter what, this is the last moment. Mu-, Mu-, Mu-!* . . . *How will all the faces of everyone look tomorrow morning when I'm not there? Surely they will look all damn serious lining up and facing each other. Someone will probably make an understanding face and say, "Poor Zuiho, she didn't have a connection with the Buddha." I should write a note: "I had to leave," and put it on the counter in the temple kitchen. Tonight I will prepare my things as much as I can so they will be easy to throw away anywhere. The bedding would be troublesome to deal with, but anyhow, I received it as a gift, so I should leave it here and go. Roshi will probably get angry and might burn such a futon.*

Suddenly I thought about Roshi—those eyes. During night sitting, she would get up even at 1 or 2 a.m. to urge me on. *Why am I worried about such a thing? I have decided, and there are not even a few hours left. Alright, this is the last few pushes of Mu in my life. I don't know how long this practice will go on, but I will try to continue it, putting my life on the line as much as I can, without any rest, throwing away everything, wrenching out my last voice. . . .*

This was on the fourth day of sesshin. Eventually I stopped thinking even those thoughts, forgetting all judgments. Letting go of it all, I painfully, recklessly practiced *Mu-, Mu-, Mu-!* I didn't even have a spare moment to notice that all my tears and sweat had dried. I was without any thoughts, single-minded.

At one point I must have been wholeheartedly voicing *Mu* when—*Whack!*—*Was that the blow of great compassion? The life-taking sword of great compassion? Truly, this was the action of the Buddha!* The sound soaked into my whole body and mind and didn't leave me. From that moment, in the door I had been staring into intensely, as if to make a hole with my eyes, a circle opened that grew bigger and bigger before me and stretched out endlessly as I continued *Mu-, Mu-, Mu-!*, limitlessly stretching out. *Mu-, Mu-, Mu-!* piercing through my whole body and mind, reverberating everywhere. *Mu-, Mu-, Mu-!* It expanded without limits, vertically and horizontally, clearly in the ten directions, expanding, filling the whole universe. I chased this expansion with my eyes wide open, straining my whole body and whirling in the middle of the expansion. It seemed in this instant everything was transparent. In the instant when again I received the kyosaku—*Whack!*—I broke through.

It is Mu, it is Mu! Everything is Mu! Zuiho is Mu! I was drowning and dying in *Mu* such that I had a hard time breathing. *How painful! How painful!*—*Mu-, Mu-!* Expanding, expanding, growing, growing—*it is all Mu!* Sweat, tears, and the joy of *Mu* were making me intoxicated. *Everything is Mu! It is Mu that fills all heavens and earth. It is expanding limitlessly, and its brightness is beyond control.* I continued to squeeze out *Mu-, Mu-!* with a hollow voice. *But what should I do with the smile that is welling up on its own? What should I do with the deep joy that is flowing from and into my chest without end? What is this emptiness, transparent like a thin silk and shining vividly?* This richness welled up and filled my whole body. It felt electric. *It is truth, love, beauty, Zen, joy . . . How heartrending is this activity of heaven and earth! The absolute world of Mu stretches out infinitely under the brilliantly shining July sunlight. Outside the window, the small flowers that until now I would just glance casually over—their freshness finally penetrated into my eyes! A dearness and loveliness of black soil that I could kiss!*

The swinging of green bamboo, the clouds passing in the sky—in everything I was able to discover my own life, burning and flickering, moving like fire. Roshi's gaze pierced my eyes, which were drowning in joy, and she said, "Your eyes are still wild. Sit steadily some more or you will become mad with *Mu.*" *Mu—it is the marvelous existence of the truth of emptiness! Even if my eyes are wild, it is okay; now the sun has risen in my cold mind! Everything that I see, everything that touches me, is truth jumping out from being trapped in a shell of concepts. . . .*

Human life is not an imagined concept, not a theory. Each step, each instant, is an act that transcends life and death; just action itself. As long as a little bit of self remains, it won't be realized. Only when we negate all of it and pierce through the self until the very bottom, then everything becomes vividly restored.

The voices of the great sage Shakyamuni and all ancestors and teachers resound continuously in my chest, welling up. The taste of the fruit I received for putting my life on the line is truly sacred. If you won't put your life on the line to pick it, you won't be able to taste the reality.

Gassho.

Nagasawa Roshi and nuns during work practice in the late 1930s.

10

FOUNDATION OF PEACE

Ms. Toshiko Nakamura

I HAD BEEN WORKING in education for seven years when I lost my younger brother and my father. Being faced two times with this parting from the physical body, I began to think intensely about the mystery of life and the question of the spirit. I wasn't satisfied just cheerfully going through my days. I came to believe that if I couldn't get to the source that lies beneath all the logic, morality, philosophy, religion, and science in this great universe, then no matter how much I was blessed with material goods and family, it would all end in vain. Yet I didn't know the best way to solve this problem. Fortunately I was able to join a sesshin at Kannon-ji training nunnery in Mitaka where I hoped I would find a guide with the key to resolving all my questions.

As I was preparing body and mind for sesshin, I prayed to the gods and buddhas for protection, asking them to help me awaken. With each day, my determination for do-or-die practice—and certain success—strengthened itself. Finally, as I was departing, I looked one last time at the faces of my mother and siblings, and I resolved that if I did not awaken, I would never enter my house again.

At the nunnery, all the nuns, including the Venerable Abbess, were wearing working clothes, preparing everything for sesshin. On seeing the serene face of the Abbess, I felt encouraged. During the formal tea, we were given detailed rules and guidelines to follow during sesshin.

In short,

1. Be earnest and set yourself for certain victory.
2. Absolutely no speaking.
3. The meals are simple; often just cold barley rice, so be prepared to fast.
4. Each person has responsibilities during the retreat. As soon as you finish your chores, go sit.
5. The daily schedule: Wake up at 3 a.m., bedtime at 9 p.m., and between—except for meals, work period, and chanting—the vast majority of the day is sitting zazen.

Four nuns were running everything under the guidance of the Abbess, so they had quite a lot of work, to the point that I felt bad for them. I was assigned to wipe down a part of the zendo in the morning and evening, and to sweep the garden. I went to bed early to rest before the start of this busy schedule, and I was amused by the well-behaved way in which I lay down and stretched out my legs and arms.

At 3 a.m., the wake-up bell rang. We opened the window and picked up our bedding and quickly put it away. *Ok, let's sit!* I thought, going to my place. I began breathing deeply from the bottom of my belly. Black figures were already quietly sitting in line. The kyosaku was circling the zendo—*Whack!* The sound reverberated in the dim space. Involuntarily, my spine straightened. I was getting increasingly nervous. I got hit on my right shoulder and it hurt, but the next moment my heart started to pound and the blood inside my body started to flow very fast. I felt refreshed, as if the great effort had started. I completely forgot my sleepiness and the itchiness of mosquitos biting my face and hands, and I continued my practice in earnest.

The night sky started to brighten. Gradually I heard cicadas and sounds from the neighboring houses. I was already sweating. The sounds of chanting, bells, and *mokugyo* (percussion instrument) blended clearly and beautifully into the sounds of nature. There was dew glistening on the plants, making them shine in the morning light.

When the signal for the morning meal came, I silently went to my seat. *"The first morsel is to cut off all evil. The second morsel is to practice all virtues. The third morsel is to liberate all sentient beings, so we all together attain the Buddha Way."* Out of the many meal sutras we chanted, this one in particular touched my heart. Until now, I had eaten food unconsciously. Here it became something to be grateful for. I reflected on how we casually say things like, "This is tasty. That is not tasty." Instead, I went beyond discrimination and complaints and prostrated myself to the things I was receiving. The problem of nutrition and amounts of food completely disappeared.

I thought about how buddhas and ancestors had left such a truly precious path for future generations, how Zen is the true foundation for establishing peace, and that now, in the wake of the terrible war, is the time for the whole nation to practice Zen. I wholeheartedly put my palms together in gassho.

I was practicing sincerely, but because of the worldliness that had permeated deeply into my mind and the marrow of my bones, it was not going well. Even when my body was sitting, my head kept thinking and my mind kept playing. Whenever I went to dokusan, I was able to be calm and focused, but somehow I just wasn't getting it at all. I feared that, as things were going, without cutting off my finger or my arm like great teachers of the past had done, the marvelous virtue, the genuine self, would not appear.

While taking a bath I looked and saw that my right shoulder was swollen. I was sad and irritated but thought to myself, *After all, practice is not easy.* In the bath the sign "Silence" glared at me. After the bath, I repeated my three prostrations at the bathhouse altar. Bowing all day and all night; in the bath and in the toilet; toward the water well, the pot, the tatami, one match, one tree, or a single blade of grass—this was the life of a nun. Their bearing was natural, simply noble. All of the nuns in training were young women. They wore black robes, and there was not a single decoration on their bodies. There was no haughtiness, no timidity—they were calm and polite, and they had an inviolable dignity. They were practicing for the liberation of all beings—what a vow to live by! It made me think about the greatness of the Dharma. When a nun kneeled in front of the toilet to clean it, polishing as if it were precious furniture, it made me bow my head and see the toilet anew. I could no longer think of the toilet as being dirty. How clearly I was being shown an example of the spirit I was looking for in myself!

The first day ended. Increasingly my thoughts became a circle of confusion, and my muscles ached as if all the bones in my body had come loose. I resolved to sit all through the night, but instead, holding *Mu*, I fell asleep.

When the wake-up bell rang above my head, I jumped to my feet, thinking, *Today, I will destroy this bag of delusion!* I vowed to the spirit of my father that I would have kensho or I would not return to the world or to teaching in school. Grinding my teeth, I went to my seat. As if prophesying the day's heat, the cicadas were already singing. *I don't get it. I look for it, I pray, but still I don't get it.* I encouraged myself not to be a coward hoping to be saved by someone else when truth lay within me. Before I knew it, together with the nun sitting next to me, we were growling frighteningly in our koan practice. The voice of the Abbess fell on us from behind: "It's hot, it's itchy, it hurts—the tears, the sweat, the drool, the snot—embrace all of it and sit! You are sitting on a *zabuton* (a mat for sitting during meditation) under a roof. The wind can come in from all directions. Compared to people who work under the scorching sun, this is nothing!"

That evening, sweeping the garden, I again became discouraged. Dark clouds of uncertainty gathered in my chest until gradually I was unable to move. I knew that there was an ancestor who, while sweeping the garden, had heard the sound of a small pebble hitting bamboo and had attained enlightenment. I chided myself not to be careless for even a moment; that when holding a broom, eating or drinking, in the toilet, while walking—just stay with *Mu*. But still, a voice in my heart said, *There must be some methods that are gentler. Isn't it enough to spend enjoyable days?* And then another voice said, *You coward! Weren't you dissatisfied with those days before coming to this temple? Didn't you come here prepared to die? Until you awaken, don't even think of leaving!*

The faces of the nuns were pure seriousness. *Practicing for the liberation of all beings, they probably never gave into this kind of cry-baby disposition,* I thought. *I am such a coward without a Bodhi-mind, but then standing in front of the children when I teach, or in front of my parents and siblings, I put on airs. How pathetic and regrettable. I am worse than these rocks in the garden!*

In dokusan, the Venerable Abbess, from whom nothing could be hidden, read my mind and yelled energetically, "Regretful and pathetic is not enough. You must become even more and more regretful!"

On the morning of the third day, it rained—rain that both humans and plants were craving. "Today is a good day. Don't be weaker than the sound of the rain. Do it!" the Abbess urged us, and we growled with such a voice that even a lion would have been ashamed. In the breaks between the rain, we could hear the voices of neighborhood children imitating us: "*Muuuu! Muuuu!*"

During kinhin after the first round of zazen, as I was quietly walking around the zendo, a new courage welled up in me and the numbness in my legs disappeared. But still, the sound of the rain, the birds singing, the cars passing by, the sound of an airplane—none of it induced a breakthrough. "You are not making enough effort. Your karma isn't ready yet!" said the Abbess in that day's teisho. Thinking about it, I realized what a lazy attitude I had, hoping for kensho in three, or even ten, days.

In the afternoon I rushed in for zazen, and all the black figures were already sitting in silence. My throat was hoarse, and I couldn't make any sound. Lamentably I invoked the spirit of my father, praying for kensho, and tears started to flow down my cheeks. The Abbess spoke with sharp words: "For how long are you going to be trapped in this five-feet-long bag of shit? Become serious!" As I received her compassionate kyosaku, my tears flowed without end. I gathered all the energy in my body, and strangely, from the bottom of my belly, a powerful growl came out. A cold sweat poured down my back while I continued working on the koan. For a while everything became like a dream, and I didn't know if this voice I heard was me or if I was this voice. In that state—*Whack!*—I got hit. And in that very moment, everything disappeared.

The Abbess simply said, "Do not form a nihilistic conception of vacancy."[25] I had to start anew, and I wondered how I could find the strength. The three small meals we had each day left me feeling hungry, and I was unable to find any more energy to make an effort.

Then, already, it was the fourth day. The Abbess cautioned us, "The first three days are like walking up a hill, the second three days are like going downhill, and they will pass very quickly. If you don't have kensho today, you won't be able to get it at all. Don't think that you will ever have another opportunity in this lifetime! Throw away this body and your delusions all at once and dive in!" Suddenly I wasn't tired at all, and there was no question of having or not having energy. Forgetting the heat, I focused on the koan, and I was surprised what kind of power appeared in me.

Finally, at the sound of the kyosaku, I broke through. When I opened my eyes, everything was *Mu*. The wooden wall in front of my eyes became so intimate, like buddhas and ancestors, like my father, like my mother and siblings. From the bottom of my chest, something hot welled up—gratitude, happiness—I couldn't help but cry and cry. How deeply moved I was at that moment, and I bowed my head.

As I was waiting to go for dokusan, the pain and tiredness suddenly flowed through my body as if a river had broken a dam. In this state of mind, as I sat silently waiting, everything I had read or heard about morality or philosophical problems became nothing more than trivial matters. *Truly, this is not a theory. It is the great reality. It Is Here*—the feeling was gradually getting deeper, and an uncontainable happiness welled up.

Surely, the Venerable Abbess will be happy, I thought as I went to see her. Instead, the complete peace of mind I had was stripped away from me. She told me that what I was so happy about was as small as a handful of sand in the great sea. "Don't be careless. Go back to your practice," she encouraged me. I was so grateful to receive those words, as this light I had found kept growing brighter and brighter. Returning to my place, I was able to sit with undivided attention, and the more I sat, the more the light expanded, growing deeper.

"Non-duality of self and other," "One is everything," "Not increasing nor decreasing, no old age, no death,"—all the words I had heard

and memorized floated through my head. These ideas became my own, and I was able to taste them. Practicing, then contemplating, then observing the circumstances, then back to practice. Repeating this many, many times, I was gradually able to find what is certain. I understood that the world of reality is so deep and so vast, that no matter how many times we verify it, we are not able to exhaust its limitlessness. I am so glad that I was one of the fortunate ones who was able to meet this great Dharma.

The hardship of my past experiences disappeared like frost under the morning sun. Both the *Heart Sutra* and the fundamental truth about creating peace have their foundation in this realization. In this, I discovered the true purpose of education. I have come to know the preciousness of my work, and I have been able to discover great hope in it. The fact that I didn't have to lose any part of my body but just had to realize something sitting on a zabuton is so precious. Now I will take this koan into my life, practicing it and cultivating it in action.

Gassho.

11

FORMLESS JEWEL

Rev. Shudo Sato

SOME FIFTEEN YEARS AGO, on a particularly clear and crisp fall day, two Dharma friends and I went out for takuhatsu. As we walked, receiving alms from the houses in each village, we marveled at the pear trees in the gardens bathing in beautiful fall sunshine, the trees' thin branches almost breaking under the weight of their fruit. I was moved by the mystery and awe of it, and as I stopped and stood in front of one pear, my eyes filled with tears. Even now—after many years have passed—I can still recall the beauty and wonder of that moment.

As my Dharma friends walked on, chanting a sutra, I followed, lost in deep contemplation. I was thinking about how that pear was doing its part perfectly, while I, with the precious karma to put on robes and become a monastic, was full of dissatisfaction, unhappiness, and innumerable fears. At that moment, the aspiration to learn about the true way of home-leaving arose in me.

The following year, I graduated from the nuns' seminary. My Dharma friends and I promised to make a zealous effort to guide women and girls as we returned to our hometowns. While

I wanted to continue my monastic education, the villagers my home temple served considered my studies as complete. But for a home leaver, the nuns' seminary is like elementary school—just the beginning. *Shouldn't a monastic's education be more than this?* I thought.

"Abbess, I am back, thank you very much" was my quiet greeting to my ordination teacher when I returned. She said, "Good grief! At last I can be at ease about this temple. I have waited for this day for a long time!" As always, the eyes of this strong-willed old nun were filled with light. Seeing that, I felt pain and sadness, as if I were being pulled into some kind of darkness. The day before, I had been discussing with my Dharma friends our hopes for the future—but my teacher was already eighty-five years old. My Dharma friends were always full of energy, striving for their future goals, but what should I do? *While my teacher is still healthy, I should ask to go—even for a year, or for half a year—to where some of my Dharma friends had gone, to Hosshin-ji.* Although I knew it was impossible, I timidly asked. My teacher and I cried together, and I gave up on this dream.

My teacher was getting older—ninety-two, ninety-three—but except for poor hearing and lower back pain, she was very healthy. Whenever someone in the village would die, she would pray to Jizo Bodhisattva, asking, "Take me too before the farmers become too busy again with work." I can still clearly remember her radiant face while chanting the Jizo mantra. Finally, at the old age of ninety-four, she peacefully passed on to the other world as if falling asleep. Together with three other nuns, I chanted the *Sutra of Bequeathed Teachings*, but I was crying so hard that I was unable to chant. I held the thirty-fifth-day's and forty-ninth-day's ceremonies. There were regular visitors to the temple, and for a while it was all fine, but when the hot summer had passed, my old dream started to gradually reappear.

I decided to go to Hosshin-ji for the November sesshin. A nun friend came by train from two hours away to house-sit for me at the end of October. Full of gratitude, I boarded the train to Obama.

Anxiety, dread, and shame took hold of my chest as I entered the nuns' changing room at Hosshin-ji. With five other nuns, I listened to the sesshin rules and guidelines. On the first, second, and third days, I received extremely meticulous instructions and kind cautions about zazen. From the fourth day, I had dokusan. As it was my first sesshin, and as I was a guest, I continued to practice counting and following the breath. On that note, my first sesshin ended.

At the end of each day we listened to the chant, "Respectfully I say to this gathering, great is the matter of life and death, impermanence is swift, each of you has to awaken, respectfully I urge you not to waste your time."[26] Whenever I heard those verses, from the bottom of my belly, the tears welled up. They were tears of repentance for battling with deluded thoughts all day long and not being able to win. That first sesshin made me repent for the times I had regretted being a monastic. At the same time, it made me aware of what kind of merit I had right now. I deeply wished for all the nuns who were full of unhappiness and dissatisfaction to be able to experience this precious, blessed monastery while they were still young.

I returned to Hosshin-ji for the rohatsu sesshin. On the third day I received the koan *Mu*, and I was happy. The war between *Mu* and deluded thoughts went on for days, but every time during dokusan I was told, "You are not serious enough." After 10 p.m., at the end of the schedule, I would sit one or two more periods. At midnight, 1 a.m., or 2 a.m., the whole mountain behind Hosshin-ji howled with *Mu-, Mu-, Mu-!* in a voice not of this world that seemed to move heaven and earth. At the end of sesshin, there was a ceremony for people who had had kensho.

Rev. Shudo Sato during the Abbess
Installation Ceremony at Chido-an, ca. 1954.

Afterward, filled with deep emotion, I embarked on a train and headed back to my hometown.

The following year, in March and April, there were three great Dharma events held at Hosshin-ji—lectures on *Shushogi*, precepts ceremony, and sesshin. At that time, I was able to meet the Venerable Abbess of the nuns' training monastery for the first time, and it was the greatest joy and honor. I prayed morning and night that the day would come when I could train at Kannon-ji nuns' training monastery.

Finally I asked the people who had helped me the most—the temple supporters and a nun from the nearby village—for permission to leave. I begged them to let me go to Tokyo for two or three years, promising that I would come back and conduct ceremonies each year during the Bon festival and New Year. As the nun from the next village understood the preciousness of true Dharma, she explained it to the temple supporters, who were complaining about my request, and was able to persuade them. That's how my vow finally came to fruition. I experienced a joy that could not be compared to anything. I became a person of floating cloud and flowing water.[27]

At the monastery, I passed the three-day *tangazume* (meditation period before entering training) and had a face-to-face meeting with Roshi. She was even more majestic than when I had met her at Hosshin-ji.

I did the October and November sesshins. When the December sesshin came, during *gyocha* (monastery practice of drinking tea) we were told, "This time, please practice hard. You are brave soldiers on the front line of the Dharma battle. If anyone dozes off, I will either hit you or throw water on you—I don't care if the tatami gets wet!" Rohatsu sesshin was that fierce.

On the third day, Roshi hit me with the kyosaku—*Whack! Whack!*—and said to the *ino* (an officer in a Zen temple), "Fill a bucket with water and bring it here. If she is sleeping, pour it over her head—this is true kindness!"

The fourth and fifth days passed, but no matter what I did, I couldn't completely dive in. *How can I become really serious? What does it mean to become really serious?* I felt worthless and pathetic, and sometimes I cried during teisho. A few times when I came back from the morning dokusan in the middle of chanting, I was heaving with sobs. I was hit with the kyosaku and admonished, "It's not the time for crying—hold on to *Mu*, just completely hold on to *Mu!*"

On day six, Roshi pulled me aside. I followed her, and she whispered, "Look at that, this is how you should do it." She pointed at Mrs. Hirose, a sixty-five-year-old woman who was our temple supporter. She was completely red like a Dharma protector, sweat was dripping from the back of her neck on this cold day. Instantly I put my hands in gassho.

Returning to my seat, I clenched my fists and sat. The bell rang for dokusan. I went and was sent away. Again I went and was sent away. Tears, snot, sweat—everything was becoming one. *Mu-, Mu-, Mu-!* I was so confused, I had to be reminded to bow when I came in. I thought maybe I had just become one with *Mu*, but that was not the case. When I gave 100 percent of my power, again the bad karma would give 100 percent of its power. Doing that sesshin, for the first time I understood the ugliness, filthiness, and awfulness of my own mind. I was astonished at how strange a thing a human being is.

The seventh day—the last day of dokusan. As always, I was attacked with, "Show me *Mu!*" But I was unable to utter a single sound. "You coward!" *Whack!!* I was forced by one of the senior nuns to go to dokusan again. "So, how is it?" She was investigating me closely, and no matter what I would do, no matter what I would say, I was sent out again. The next dokusan, the instant

I got hit by Roshi with the kyosaku—I started laughing. At that time, Roshi also grinned broadly. Her smile is still clearly engraved in my memory. For three years I had never seen her smile like that.

We ate sweet porridge. Afterward there was a kensho confirmation ceremony for Mrs. Hirose, and then we had tea. Ah, the taste of that tea! For people after a week of sesshin, it was so delightful, as if we were drinking tea for the very first time. Instantly forgetting all the hardships from the week, we ate, talked, and laughed. This experience cannot be compared to anything worldly.

Time passed, and as the war intensified, I was not allowed to leave my temple. There were regular evacuations from Tokyo. The war was getting worse for us, but I wanted to go back to Tokyo, as I was full of deep questions: *Once the bomb falls, isn't human body just ash? And if one doesn't quickly grasp the formless treasure, what is the use of having been born?*

Before I went to the nuns' training monastery, I had received a letter from the Venerable Daiun Sogaku Harada Roshi, saying, "For a monastic, no matter what skills you have, if you don't awaken, you are of no help to people. But even if you have no skills, and you awaken, you are a worthy monastic. I think I will be healthy for the next two or three years, so please do the training well and come for a visit." *No matter what someone says, I should just go,* I thought. *After all, if I have to die, isn't it better to die together with Dharma friends practicing true Dharma under the guidance of a Zen master?*

As I said farewell to Jizo Bodhisattva and Kannon Bodhisattva at the main altar, I resolved that I wouldn't return to my home temple, Chido-an, until I had kensho, vowing to die together with everyone else. Without listening to the temple supporters who tried to stop me, I arrived in Tokyo for the third time.

Luckily I didn't encounter any air raids, and I arrived safely at the nuns' training monastery. Like everyone, I was grateful that the nunnery continued to do sesshin, not stopping until our neighborhood was bombarded.

In September 1945, we had a sesshin commemorating the end of the war, and we continued to hold sesshin every month. At the next year's sesshin, our *tenzo* (monastery cook) had kensho. It happened after nine years of hardships, so everyone's joy was more than usual. In my heart I also vowed to do the same. Counting all of the sesshins I had done—a few dozen by then—I was wondering when I would finally awaken. I had bad karma, this I knew. But I also knew, even if only a little, the preciousness of the Dharma and the blood and tears shed in hardship by our noble ancestors.

I did my best in February and March, but it was as before. During the March sesshin I was urged, "You have endured so much, you should have had kensho by now. But the fact that you cannot means that you are not sufficiently relying on the buddhas and ancestors and that you have forgotten your deceased teacher." After that, when I prayed—*Buddhas of Chido-an, please, look at this tearful Shudo*—suddenly the buddhas started to appear.

Again, the April sesshin came. Compared to how long a week felt in the beginning of my practice, now the time passed quickly. Distracted thoughts only came up occasionally. The flower vase and the incense burner before my seat seemed to be smiling affectionately.

In dokusan on the seventh day I was asked, "Did you sit last night?" I replied, "I did not." "You didn't sit—you just sleep when you want to sleep, eat when you want to eat, not thinking about kensho, making light of buddhas and ancestors? How disgusting. You're not even worth the kyosaku." *Ding, ding*—I was sent out. After that, everyone got the kyosaku but me. Some would even get seven or eight blows; it was quite relentless. I knew I could not do night sittings, but I decided to sit after meals and during breaks instead.

Then came the 3 p.m. dokusan. How many times was I ousted and ousted again from this dokusan room? Until, in one instant, when the Venerable Abbess said, "This is it!"—I woke up from the dream. I broke through.

This time it was laughter that filled the universe; it was *Mu*. I jumped at Roshi, then suddenly came back to myself, and my body was so light. During evening chanting it felt as if the sound was reaching Chido-an. Flowing without hindrance, it reached the whole universe. I prostrated, flooded with emotion.

The next day, even though an extreme food shortage was imminent, they cooked celebratory rice with red beans for me. The Venerable Abbess and all my Dharma friends prepared everything as if just for me, and I was moved to tears. The Venerable Abbess said, "Because you didn't go back on New Year and did your best, you were able to do it." Although I must have caused so much trouble for everyone, it was worth it. Now I will repay what I have received: *Sentient beings are numberless, I vow to save them.* I will live this vow. I am so happy, so grateful.

Soon after kensho I went to Mitaka by bicycle for some errands. The year before I had been scared when I had to ride even less than one mile, but this year, although it was the first time I went this far, I was not afraid in the slightest. Even in places with a lot of people, I was just calm and easy—it was a great feeling. It is as Dogen Zenji said, "If you attain this point, you are like a dragon entering the water, like a tiger taking to the mountain."[28] Tears flowed, I was so happy. In the past, a widow had donated to me a precious gift, and it was one of the reasons I had become a practicing novice—to be a nun that could receive such a thing without shame. Now I could gladly chant a sutra for her deceased husband. The main Buddha at Chido-an, all of the temple supporters, the nun from a nearby village—I have only gratitude for all of them. Once we are born as human beings, without fail we will go through hardships in one way or another. If we are already suffering, we should turn to the true Dharma, to truth, to endure all hardships. Whatever has shape will without fail be destroyed, but this formless jewel is ours for life after life, world after world.

All of you virtuous nuns and women—there is a practice place where you can dig up this formless jewel. It is in Tokyo prefecture, in the town of Mitaka—please remember that.

The Venerable Roshi of Kannon-ji is always, always using the hands of Kannon Bodhisattva, giving her all for the liberation of all beings.

A polished self is like a radiant jewel
Preciousness of the Dharma shining through the three worlds.

Gassho.

12

EVENING STARS

Ms. Mieko Tanaka

AFTER I LOST MY HUSBAND in October 1948, all my happiness was destroyed. Loneliness crept into my body and mind. The days were miserable, and having no one to rely on, I wondered if I would completely break down.

At a memorial service for my husband, I made the acquaintance of a nun from the neighborhood. We met a second time, and a third time. With each meeting my affection for her grew, and I looked forward to the days she would come and visit, more than anything else. Each time I would listen to her, I started to think that I would like to try to do sesshin at Chido-an in Nigorikawa.

In May, my karmic affinity with Dharma ripened, and I was able to attend sesshin. For the first two days I was just happy and grateful to be allowed to attend the retreat. As I didn't know left from right, I just followed what Nagasawa Roshi said. On the evening of the third day, I was given the koan *Mu*. As I followed the practice of *Mu*, I started to feel acutely the depth of the sins I had committed. While sitting on my zabuton, I didn't know what to do with myself. Day after day I continued to cry. After three days

I felt like my body and mind were being purified by the tears. This first sesshin finished with just continued repentance. Even so, I thought of it with gratitude, putting my hands together in gassho.

Later that month I attended a series of lectures on *Shushogi* at Chigetsu-ji. After listening to those deep teachings, I truly felt that I must awaken, and I etched this intention on the bottom of my heart. To prepare for the upcoming October sesshin, I went once a month to Ms. Nakayama's house for a longer sitting, to tighten my slacking mind.

October came. I settled my business and family affairs so as to have no regrets, and once more I departed for sesshin.

From the beginning, I entered with a life-or-death resolve. The Abbess told us, "Don't count on there being another sesshin!" In my heart I made a firm resolution not to miss this opportunity. However, during the first day, even though I sat up straight and my mouth was practicing *Mu* out loud, my mind was distracted. I completely did not understand this practice of *Mu*. The dokusan bell rang a few times, but I was unable to go, and finally the day was coming to an end. At the evening dokusan I received various instructions from the Venerable Abbess, many of which struck me deeply, and I regretted wasting this day. I went back to my seat thinking, *Tomorrow without fail I will do it!*

On the second day, I came into dokusan in a rush, and Roshi told me, "If you fall into haste, you will fall back." After doing some strong breathing from the bottom of my belly, doing *Mu* out loud together with her, I finally calmed down.

During the afternoon free sitting time, I was resting a little, thinking it pointless to sit when I was so tired and had so many thoughts. Suddenly I was hit on my side, and I heard Ms. Nakayama's voice, "What are you dawdling here for? If you don't hurry, you won't make it!" Startled, I felt ashamed of my laziness. Listening to the second day's teisho, again I made the resolution to awaken, no matter what. I told the Venerable Abbess, "Even if I have to die, I will do it!" She replied, "If you die, wouldn't you be unable to have kensho?" I responded, "Yes! I won't die before I do it!"

But although I made that vow, still I was not getting *Mu*. I began to think that no matter how far I would go, I could never reach the end of the path. I went to dokusan and got a harsh rebuke: "Because you are thinking, 'I don't get it, I don't get it,' it is all in vain." I knew that if I let myself think like that, nothing would happen, and I continued—*Mu-, Mu-, Mu-!*—desperately relying on Buddha.

While staring at a sliding door, suddenly I thought, *Ah, I can see Mu! I caught the tail of Mu!* How happy I was, seeing that there was a way forward. *This time, I am not going to let the tail go,* I thought. *Even a little moment of break would be so regrettable.* So even while walking—*Mu*; when paying a visit to the altar—*Mu-*; just *Mu-, Mu-, Mu-!* I was holding tightly onto the tail of *Mu*.

The fifth day passed quickly, and the sixth day was really difficult. I felt like I was climbing a steep mountain on the tips of my toes. I was cautioned, "If for a moment you let yourself be careless, you will fall down into the bottom of the valley!" But even just taking a breath was painful. I said, "Roshi, it feels like my chest will burst open." "Even if your chest were to burst open or your arm were to break, isn't that fine? Who said that she will do it even if she would have to die?" With that single admonition I was thrown out of the room. With a renewed desperation I practiced, my hands in gassho. Even more, I entrusted everything to Buddha and continued, *Mu-, Mu-, Mu-!* Finally the end of the day came, and praying that I wouldn't fail, I went to bed.

I didn't sleep a wink. The morning came and somehow I felt depressed. The dokusan bell rang and when I sat in front of the Venerable Abbess she said, "I am waiting for you." Her words were full of compassion. *Ah, it's more than I deserve. She cares for me that much!* I thought, and my heart lit up again.

In the middle of the morning sutra chanting, I came back from dokusan and sat at the back. I continued my koan practice and chanting sutras. Then suddenly, hearing the sound of the wall clock—*tick, tick, tick*—and at the same time, the sound of my heart pumping blood—*ton-ton, ton-ton, ton-ton*—in this instant—I forgot myself. I broke through.

It is one! It is one! Everything is Mu! I went to dokusan and finally received approval. I was so moved, so grateful, and so joyful I wanted to thank everything I came across—Buddha, Roshi, the nuns, the grasses, the trees—I was full of a sense of intimacy.

I will never forget the beauty of the stars when I looked up at that night sky. In that state of being deeply moved, just taking a bath became incredibly precious. The next morning, refreshed and with a sense of being washed and purified, I quickly returned home to where my mother, my older sister, and my dear child waited for me.

Gassho.

13

LIKE MOTHER, LIKE DAUGHTER

Ms. Shizue Tanaka[29]

WHEN I WAS FOURTEEN, I was taken in as a foster daughter by the Tanaka family. After graduating from a girls' school, I entered a dressmaking academy, and while I was studying there, my father passed away. In an instant, I went from having everything I needed to being thrust into a world of darkness. My mother and I spent day after day in an ongoing state of shock, but she had a strong will. She regained her strength and did everything for me. After I graduated from the dressmaking academy, I finished one more year of a postgraduate course. My mother always said, "Women should be obedient and gentle, and we should smile all the time," but I couldn't really do it. Instead I acted utterly selfishly.

After my father's death, my mother was drawn to Buddhism. She participated in a May sesshin, after which she started to say, "In the end, there is no other way but to do zazen." I had no idea what she was talking about. The following October, my mother had kensho. I was amazed by that. My mother had become completely different. Whenever she spoke with the Venerable Abbess, her appearance was so joyful. Sometimes she would cry, and sometimes she would laugh, but she would open her heart to talk about anything. It made me unbearably envious. I felt left out. Secretly I vowed in my heart that I too would go for sesshin someday.

September came and my marriage was arranged for the following spring. My mother said, "Will you go for the October sesshin or not? There's no way to know when you could go again once you're married." So I put aside all the commitments I had and arranged to go.

The first night of sesshin I was unable to sleep—1 a.m., 2 a.m., 3:30 a.m. The wake-up bell rang and the day started. Since I didn't know anything, I just followed other people and did whatever they did. On the first day I was taught how to practice and given the guidelines for zazen. I continued counting the breath as I had been instructed. As time passed, my legs fell asleep. I was hungry and just hoped for the time to pass quickly and the night to come.

The second day came and I was ashamed of the previous day's lazy mind. Although I started with high spirits, thinking, *Today is the day I will give it my all*, it was not going so well. Even if I wanted to forget about everything and just do the practice, I would remember various things and cry. The more I thought, *I shouldn't be thinking this kind of thing*, the more the tears would come. *My mom also suffered like this, and after that she was able to awaken. Whatever my mom could do, surely I can do too!* Although my mother had wanted to go to sesshin as well, she had stayed behind to take care of the house. I bowed my head with gratitude, thinking I should continue by any means. Just when I was thinking that, I heard a voice from behind saying, "Your mother wanted to come so much, but instead she sent you. It is not impossible to get it during the first sesshin. Just do it!"

On day three I started practicing *Mu*. My legs didn't hurt anymore, but I didn't know why I still had no energy. I started to worry about tomorrow—if I was gradually losing energy, sliding down a slippery slope . . . what would happen?

Finally the middle day came. I started to get frantic. I didn't know what I should bring into dokusan, but I knew not going would be even more painful. I went and simply said, "I have understood what a blessing my mother is." "You too must give it your all," the Abbess told me. "This will be the best gift for your mother." Her words were so kind, and I was so grateful that again the tears started to flow.

I concentrated on one point, doing *Mu-, Mu-, Mu-!* The monitor encouraged me strongly: "Even if this is your first time, if you do it, you will get it!" I was so grateful for those precious words. *Everyone is so devoted. And me, what am I doing?* I thought, and I renewed my practice with all my heart.

When the fifth day came, I was very anxious and again became quite frantic. *If I can't do it today, I cannot count on doing it tomorrow.* Just then, Mrs. Kasashima, with whom I was sharing a room, encouraged me: "You are your mother's child, aren't you? Without fail, you can do it." I went to dokusan, and when I said, "Venerable Abbess, I am my mother's child, but why don't I have willpower? Please beat me," she said, "Instead of thinking, 'Why don't I have willpower?,' just practice *Mu!*"

Returning to my place, I could hear someone next to me doing their koan in a voice full of pain. *Okay, I won't be worse than them. Mu-, Mu-, Mu-!* I heard the whispered voice of the monitor, "*Mu.*" Ah, *everything is Mu! Mu-, Mu-, Mu-!* I repeated continuously, spontaneously, without effort. *This is it!* Then when I got hit on my back—*Whack!*—at this moment, fire burst out of my eyes and the world completely changed! I broke through.

I ran to the Kannon-do, and in front of the statue of Kannon with thirty-three bodies I said, "Thank you, thank you," repeating words of gratitude and repentance. Then I yelled, "Venerable

Abbess, Venerable Abbess!" and went back to the zendo again. I didn't know what to do with myself. I clung to Ms. Nakayama and yelled, "Mom! Mom!" I went to sit in front of the Buddha altar, then I went to the kitchen and was scolded by the monitor, "Calm down! Go back and sit strongly." I returned to sitting, and my mind became quiet again.

When the bell rang for evening dokusan, I entered the room. Without any bow, I said, "I am *Mu*," and I just sat down. When I described in detail what had happened, I was told, "Calm down more and sit a bit more." I was sent back. On the sixth day I deeply quieted my mind and was able to reply to all the Venerable Abbess's questions, one after another, and she confirmed my kensho. I was so grateful. It seemed so difficult, so painful—but after I got it, it all seemed like nothing. I was so joyous, I only wanted to laugh.

On the seventh day I was told that today my mother would come to pick me up, and I was so happy that I couldn't contain myself. I hugged everyone, and I cried and cried. Of course everybody was happy for me, but when I thought how my mom would feel, I was even more overjoyed. The Venerable Abbess told me, "As you had kensho, from now on you must become a person who is good to everyone. Do not be wary of others. A person as young as you must help establish a new Japan. Also, above all, don't forget to be a splendid person and a good daughter to your mother." I etched those precious words on my heart and I looked anew into the future filled now with hope.

Gassho.

14

TRUE LIVING WAY

Rev. Bunyu Igaarashi

AFTER I GRADUATED from the nuns' seminary, I was busy at my teacher's temple for three or four years. But I kept asking myself, *Is this enough? For what purpose was I born as a human being? Why am I shaving my head and putting on robes?* I was chanting sutras that I had barely learned, I was receiving offerings and eating delicious meals prepared for me wholeheartedly. I sat on a high seat and received respect, but I didn't feel worthy of it because I wasn't at peace. *Why should I receive the efforts of people's hard work earned in sweat? What is my real duty?* I was deeply contemplating these questions.

When I thought about the purpose of the Way—to save sentient beings—and that I could not even talk about it with confidence, I felt sad and distressed. I was terrified knowing that in the next life I would have to take responsibility for this debt. I was searching for something that would help me find peace, something I could rely on.

In June 1947, I followed my teacher to Chido-an, where Nagasawa Ni-Roshi of the nuns' training monastery in Tokyo was giving teisho on *Shushogi* and leading practice for five days. In the mornings and evenings we sat zazen and did dokusan, and during the day we listened to teisho on *Shushogi*. The days were deeply meaningful and passed quickly. For the first time I understood the path that monastics should follow, and feeling a great responsibility, I made a firm resolution.

I realized that we cannot wait for someone to rebuild the country of our ancestors; each person has to do their part. For that I felt that no matter what, I had to awaken. If only I could familiarize myself with Dharma, value zazen, and do sesshin under a true teacher, then, without fail, I would be able to awaken and finally become a person of virtue, full of compassion. If I couldn't become a person of virtue, someone who could save others, then that would be the most inexcusable thing before the buddhas and ancestors. I always kept this in mind, never losing connection with it. Moving forward, I followed the teachings.

For some time, I wasn't blessed with the opportunity I had hoped for, but I was finally able to participate in as many as five sesshins. I don't know how much trouble I caused the Zen master and everyone else with my strong ego and deep sinful karma. No matter how much kyosaku I received, no matter what guidance I was given, no matter how much I was admonished, I was quite unable to have kensho. I implored the buddhas and ancestors to help me, and I cried without end.

During the November sesshin I felt increasingly anxious, awkward, ashamed, and lifeless. *Other people could do it, why can't I?* I thought. *I don't care about my life. I don't mind if I have to die to have kensho. And if I won't die, then just kill me!* I felt I couldn't shamelessly be here without getting it any longer. Forgetting about what other people thought, I started sitting desperately.

About three hours before the end of sesshin, all the pain in my body had disappeared and, utterly absorbed in it, I was just continuing my koan practice.

Finally, during the evening chanting, when I heard the sutra, I broke through—I penetrated *Mu*.

My practice had been so immature. Seeing the example of all the buddhas of the three worlds, all successive generations of ancestors and teachers' efforts, I could only repent. I prostrated myself completely in front of the buddhas and ancestors.

Who should rebuild the land of our ancestors? Having our respective duties, and combining our efforts, I pray we all try diligently to spread the true Dharma. I believe that the foundation for this is the true strength of our own virtue, and for that, the most important thing is sesshin. If a buddha's disciple is not doing sesshin, it is inexcusable before the buddhas and ancestors. I believe that if we just consume Buddha's rice, we will have to incur the Dharma punishment for it. There is no other power than ourselves to turn the decay of the Dharma into true Dharma, by doing sesshin on a large scale and creating a lot of virtuous people. Truly, today we have so many problems, it is hard to sleep. As monastics, we should first awaken to our true nature, create a real capacity within ourselves, and then join our forces, making an effort for all humankind, for all sentient beings of this world. This is what it means for religion to come alive. Buddhism—that is, sesshin—will eventually create a peaceful world. For me, true practice starts from now. I beg all of you to give me exhaustive encouragement and Dharma love.

Gassho.

15

THE JOY OF BEING SAVED

Ms. Kikuko Wakasugi

I AM AN IGNORANT old woman of seventy-three. When I was sixteen, I would vomit blood, then from my twenties onward, I had many difficult sicknesses, one after another, that in those times were considered incurable—a colon infection, lymph-node tuberculosis, intestinal tuberculosis, and a stomach ulcer. But strangely, among us six siblings, I am the only one who has survived until today, thanks only to protection from the Buddha.

When I was thirty-eight, my husband passed away, leaving me with four children. My oldest son entered Imperial University and graduated successfully. My second son died. My third son graduated from Waseda University. My first and third sons and my daughter were in good health, and I fulfilled my long-term wish to do the memorial ceremony on the thirty-third anniversary of my husband's passing.

In the harrowing time after the lost war, I felt unworthy, and I couldn't go on taking from our country without giving back. I prayed to Jizo Bodhisattva to come and take me, but although I wanted to, I couldn't die. When I contemplated the preciousness of Buddhism—thinking of the terrifying, sinful deeds I had done—I wished to become a nun in the next life and focus exclusively on the path to buddhahood.

One day I heard a talk by Sozen Nagasawa Roshi. She told the story of an *unsui* (monastic in training) from a certain monastery who was in despair. He couldn't attain kensho and had committed suicide. After that, he became a ghost, appearing in the toilet; when other unsui would come to the sink, he would pour the water over their hands for them. In the end, he was saved by the abbot of that temple. When I heard this, I was truly scared. Most of all, I started to worry, *If I cannot awaken, it would be so regrettable. If I want to be a nun in my next life, I should have kensho in this life, to plant the seed of becoming one.* I had heard the saying of an ancient teacher, "If you won't save this body in this lifetime, in what life are you going to save it?" After much reflection, I realized that by any means necessary, I had to awaken.

I felt eager to go to sesshin, but when I remembered how frail my body was and what a lazy and weak-willed person I was, I knew it wouldn't be easy to practice. Sometimes Roshi would honor me with a visit, and when I told her of my intention, she rejoiced, encouraging me and kindly teaching me the main points about practice.

Still, the anxiety of failing, of not awakening, was constantly and painfully on my mind. I thought that there was nothing else to do but seek protection from the buddhas and ancestors, and I began visiting the shrine of Fudo Myoo in the cold weather. At the shrine, I saw a *hyakudoishi* (stone for worship), so I made a vow that in twenty-one days I would step on it one hundred times, and I was able to successfully fulfill this vow. Then I visited the Kannon shrine twenty-one times. I also completed making twenty thousand Jizo stamps and did the ceremony of throwing them into water. Every day I chanted *Enmei Jukku Kannon-gyo* one thousand times, *Fudo Dharani* one thousand times, *Jizo Dharani* one thousand times, and the *Medicine Buddha Dharani* 108 times. On the days I couldn't complete these recitations, I made an effort to chant late into the night. Morning and evening without fail, I practiced zazen for one hour, and single-mindedly I prayed that my vows would come to fruition.

Finally I was confident that I could participate in sesshin, so I wrote a letter to Roshi to the address where she was visiting at the time. The answer came: "Falseness will sometimes appear, so wipe it out, and devote yourself to sitting." So, diligently I continued.

My third son brought me to the temple for sesshin. I felt deep gratitude and indebtedness for the overflowing compassion of the Venerable Abbess, and the sympathy I received from the *tanto* (senior nun responsible for training novices) and all the nuns. They were so kind that it felt almost as if I had come just for a visit, not for training, and it made me bow wholeheartedly. *To repay this blessing, the only thing to do is to awaken—until then, I won't stop even for an instant,* I thought, and I sat with all my heart.

At each dokusan, Roshi would throw me out saying, "No good, no good! You are on a one-hundred-foot pole. You must take one more step! One more breath. This is the greatest barrier." It was such hardship, such suffering, being trapped in a corner. *With an impertinent mind, forgetting my stupidity, I had come to sesshin, bringing my gray-haired head here to disgrace myself,* I thought, and keenly feeling the superficiality of the self, the tears of repentance fell down my cheeks. *But once having decided to come, if I won't follow through with my original intention no matter what, how could I face Roshi? That would be inexcusable! Kannon Bodhisattva, please save me!* I prayed single-mindedly.

One afternoon, I moved my leg three centimeters and suddenly my chronic nerve pain returned with great intensity. I looked at the wooden wall in front of me and in that instant—heaven and earth were one, everything became one—I broke through. Whatever I looked at, whatever I heard, it was *Mu*. I completed the Venerable Abbess's examination, and she confirmed I had completely penetrated the source of *Mu*, the source of the myriad things. When I received the Abbess's words—that since I had had kensho, now I could slowly do koan practice—I returned to myself as if for the first time and wondered whether it was all a dream. I was so happy, I cried as I bowed.

Now, no matter what I look at, it is all one. It is entirely thanks to the protection of Kannon Bodhisattva, all buddhas and ancestors, and the great effort of Roshi. I bow with my hands in gassho, full of deep joy.

Where did this karma for attainment come from? For the joy of receiving this supreme treasure, I don't even have the words. Before, I was closed and imprisoned in a narrow shell, and now I have taken the first step into an expansive heaven and earth. I spend my days in ease, feeling intimate with everything. Unlike others, who on top of accumulating practice have extensive learning—I am someone who cannot do anything. I am spineless and incompetent. I only vow that through limitless kalpas in the future—birth after birth, world after world, without regressing—I will be endeavoring on the Buddha Way, to express my gratitude for buddhas and ancestors, and to repay my debt to Roshi. From the bottom of my heart, I wish for all people to attain this experience, this joy of being saved, this precious state of mind.

Roshi told me to be a good grandmother, chant sutras, offer merit to establish peace, and continue my practice. I will make an effort, as she said. For the deep compassion of Roshi, and for hardships themselves, I can only wholeheartedly bow in gratitude.

Gassho, and a hundred bows.

Construction of the new zendo building, in the late 1950s.

16

REPAYING ALL BLESSINGS

Rev. Zenkai Yamauchi

FOR EIGHT YEARS, I had an aspiration that wouldn't leave me even for a moment. Finally it was fulfilled when at last I was allowed to enter training at the precious nunnery. Now I spend my days in gratitude.

In 1932, the abbess of Hankyu-ji in the town of Takaoka invited the Venerable Harada Roshi to teach there. Since then, he has come every year to teach a sesshin for the nuns in the western part of Toyama prefecture. What good fortune that I had a karmic affinity, and I was able to participate in this extremely rare sesshin, to do dokusan with Roshi—who was overflowing with compassion— and to listen to his teisho. During this time, a friend of mine two years younger than me had kensho. I was making a great effort, but no matter what I did, I was unable to awaken.

An elder Dharma sister of mine who had gone to Hosshin-ji for sesshin and had practiced at Kannon-ji told me, "Hosshin-ji surely is the peerless demon's dojo. It is quite amazing. But the nunnery is exceptionally precious. If you have Bodhi-mind after your graduation from the nuns' seminary, I will ask the Venerable Abbess to let you practice there to your heart's content." With great joy, I thanked her from the bottom of my heart.

Finally I graduated from the nuns' seminary. I pressed my Dharma sister to help me enter the nunnery, but she responded with unexpected reserve, saying, "First you have to ask our ordination teacher." I pleaded with our teacher, but she said firmly, "You are still a young, unruly kid and a careless person, and I don't trust you. You would be a nuisance for the Venerable Abbess and all of the sangha there." My whole body became hot with the flame of anger.

I became rebellious, even over small things, but after some time, from the depths of my mind, I experienced a change of attitude and began to regret my foolishness. I gave up insisting that right now is the time, although I was still single-minded about going to the training monastery. Crying myself to sleep each night, I waited for my karmic affinity with the Dharma to ripen.

One day my teacher said these blessed words: "Today, nuns should practice hard. Even the laypeople are giving their all doing zazen and polishing their character. If we monastics are just sleeping, it is inexcusable before the buddhas and ancestors, and shameful in front of laypeople. If you are determined, I will let you go to the nunnery." Without leaving enough space for a hair, I said, "Yes! I am completely determined. Please!" I made gassho, expressing my gratitude for this realization of my aspiration. My teacher sent a letter with an inquiry to the nunnery.

After three days I met up with a good friend from the nuns' seminary. I was so happy about going to the nunnery, I was unable to hide it. She was also happy, as if it was her own joy, saying, "Your wish of many years has been fulfilled. So the time is ripe. Give it your all and come back." Then she added, "But I will tell you this as a friend—that from reading some of Nagasawa Roshi's writing, it seems that this nunnery is in a temporary building that looks like a pigpen, and they are doing takuhatsu for the construction of the zendo. So if a chubby person like you will be stomping heavily while walking on those old floor boards, they might break. Or if you make some mistake, it will cause a big uproar. So be very careful. . . . "

Finally, the reply from the Venerable Abbess arrived. I took this letter and went to the nuns' seminary where my teacher worked. Before I met my teacher, some students that had been standing around in small groups surrounded me, and each person congratulated me: "Zenkai, you are going to the nunnery in Tokyo, aren't you? Congratulations!" "Please be well, practice hard, and come back." On my way back, I had to attend a memorial service at a temple, and there as well it seemed everyone had heard about it, and everybody was saying, "Stay healthy and practice hard," treating me as if I were someone noble. I felt a great responsibility had been put on my shoulders.

When my teacher and I read the letter from the Venerable Abbess, each phrase and word penetrated to the marrow of my bones; it felt somehow both frightening and precious. As my friend had warned me before, the letter said that the practice place was small and looked just like a pigpen. I recalled Shoju Ronin[30] and Hakuin Zenji[31] and thought, *Even if it is a pigpen or a stable, if it is a practice place where a world-famous nun lives—one who, through her guidance, is liberating women—what is the problem? There are grand monasteries with all seven buildings,[32] but often there is no Buddha in those golden halls. Even if this temple is small, if the people inside it are all real bodhisattvas, surely the Dharma light of true transmission is shining there.* I vowed to the buddhas and ancestors to waste not a moment and arrive there as soon as possible to participate in the great joy of going for takuhatsu for the construction of a new zendo.

Finally the time to enter the training came. I had been saving money to go to the nunnery for a long time. When my teacher

Takuhatsu to raise funds for the building of the new zendo, ca. 1950.
Rev. Zenkai Yamauchi is in the second row, second from the left.

gave me money for a train ticket, I would walk instead and save ten or twenty sen.[33] If I received a little money from someone, I would also save it. All the savings from ten to forty sen had added up to fifty yen. The day would soon be here that eleven years of savings could finally see the sun.

One morning in late November, I arrived at Kissho-ji train station, not knowing absolutely anything. Gathering my courage, I went to the station worker and asked, "How do I get to the town of Mitaka?" An elegant woman, a teacher about twenty-seven years old, was standing by my side, and after looking me over, from the top of my head to the tip of my toes, she said, "Are you going to practice in the temple in Mitaka?" "Yes, that is right," I replied. "In that case, you should take this bus," and together we got on a blue bus. After some time, the bus stopped at Shinagawa. The teacher kindly and respectfully said, "Alright, Miss Nun, let's get off here. I will accompany you as my school is on the way to the nunnery." She walked together with me, taking fast, small steps. "Where did you come from?" she asked. "From Ecchu Province," I replied. The teacher's face looked impressed. When we reached the school, she said politely, "Well, Miss Nun, I will leave you here. Keep going straight. If you need directions, ask someone again for help. Please take care of your body and do your training." She bowed and went quickly into the school. I went on toward the nunnery, following the big asphalt road, with a question rising in my mind: *What kind of person is Nagasawa Roshi?*

Before I knew it, I came to a shrine for Jizo Bodhisattva and wondered, *Perhaps this is the nunnery.* I looked through the gap on the side of the shrine and saw a sign written in large letters: Nuns' Training Monastery. In my heart I yelled, *This is it!* but then instantly my whole body and mind got nervous. When I went to the front of the monastery, I noticed that it was completely different from what I had been imagining back home. It was a small temple, but the plants and flowers in the garden looked so beautiful, somehow graceful—giving a wordless Dharma sermon—and my body and mind felt relieved. Slowly I went and stood in front of the entrance, caught my breath, then faced the *han* and hit one, two, three times. I kept carefully breathing, and I waited. My eye caught the letters written on the han:

One grain of rice offered by a faithful donor,
Is as heavy as Mount Sumeru,
If you won't attain the Way,
You will be reborn with fur and horns.

I bowed my head low, saying, "Yes, I understand."

I hit the han three times again. After a short time, the nun responsible for guests gently opened the paper-screen door and asked me several questions. Usually I have a heart of steel, but my body was shaking. Inside, I was begging the Buddha on the main altar to let me stay.

I successfully completed the three-day tangazume, and I received permission to enter the training. I made three prostrations to the main altar to give thanks for the fulfillment of my wish, and I went to bow and have my first face-to-face meeting with the Venerable Abbess. I was honored to receive many kind and compassionate words that touched my heart, and I took them deeply in. I vowed to the Buddha to, by all possible means, stay for ten years in training.

On the same day, rohatsu sesshin started. *It is the last great Dharma battle of the year. How lucky I am that right after entering the zendo, I am able to take part in this rarest and most-difficult-to-encounter great Dharma battle,* I thought, and I went to my seat clutching my fists. I was told to continue with the koan *Mu* that I had received from Harada Roshi.

Zazen, dokusan, teisho—every day repeated. My body was tired, I didn't understand *Mu*, and my mind was panicking. I went to dokusan and I was scolded: "You are making a theory out of *Mu*. You can't understand *Mu* with logic." From a young age, I had the habit of theorizing and arguing, and I had often been scolded by my teacher and older Dharma sisters for that. Deeply in my heart, I apologized: *Ah, Venerable Abbess, I am sorry for not being straightforward. From now on, I will absolutely not use logic and honestly become Mu.* While fighting with makyo, the days were passing in vain. I could only sigh. *What a waste. I spent one whole week in Buddha's house without realizing it.*

I had understood the theory that everything is *Mu*, but somehow I couldn't really agree with it. Finally the ango finished and at the end of it, we chanted the hymn of the nunnery and danced.

When the first sesshin of the new training period came and the Venerable Abbess said the precious words, "Everyone, give it your all," I firmly vowed to the buddhas and ancestors that during this sesshin, even if I were to die, I would not get up until I had had kensho and attained the Way.

Day one, day two—gradually the final day approached. The skin of this balloon of delusion was firm and not breaking. Every time I went to dokusan, I heard the words, "Horns of duality are still working too much," and—*Whack! Whack!*—she would break those horns of delusional thinking with the kyosaku of the buddhas and ancestors. *How precious!* I would bow and go back to the dokusan bell area, where I would meet Ino *Osho* (a formal title for a nun or monk), who would send me back again: "Go to dokusan one more time." I would go and bow in front of the Venerable Abbess—*Whack! Whack!*—*ring, ring, ring*—*Mu*. I would leave, and again I was sent back in. This repeated around four or five times. How my ghost-looking eyes were full of bitter tears of repentance! I went to dokusan again. "Wash your whole body and mind with those tears and come back." *Whack! Whack!*—I did my bow, forgetting myself. I was desperately doing *Mu-, Mu-, Mu-! Ah, because of my bad karma from limitless past kalpas, no matter how many years pass, I cannot do it. Ah, what can I do? I should repent and repent,* I thought, until exhausted in body and mind, I couldn't even voice *Mu* out loud.

The last dokusan started. *I shouldn't lose heart,* I thought. *I should do my best until the last minute, Mu-, Mu-, Mu-.* From somewhere courage rose up in me, and I hit the dokusan bell in a daze. Before I knew it, I was sitting before the Venerable Abbess. She held up the kyosaku and said something—I didn't hear clearly what she said—but in that instant *I got it, I got it!*—I broke through.

For a moment I was so overjoyed, it was as if I went crazy. With the Venerable Abbess in front of me, in tears, I put my hands together and bowed and bowed. "It is me, it is me, Venerable Abbess. It is me," I repeated over and over. After a while, the Venerable Abbess said, "Calm down!" And I sat up straight again. The Venerable Abbess asked me various questions about *Mu*, then she gave me teachings, explaining that the ceremony of kensho confirmation is just the first step in practice; that afterward, great effort is needed. If with great care, like looking for a needle in a haystack, I practiced wholeheartedly, then the Dharma would transform me and I would be able to proceed, heading upward to seek Bodhi and downward to transform sentient beings.

I had heard these kinds of words before, and although I had agreed with them, they hadn't sunk in. But after attaining the state of mind of *Mu*, for the first time these words truly became engraved in my heart. The many things I had learned during my time in the nuns' seminary that had felt so difficult to grasp at the time were one after another appearing with clarity in my mind. What I hadn't understood, now I was able to know. *How blessed with Dharma I am!* I was able to enter this extremely rare and difficult-to-encounter temple and practice until my heart's content under the wings of this precious Venerable Abbess. *Ah, how grateful!* It was thanks to my ordination teacher, as well as to my elder Dharma sister. I faced the northern sky and vowed to repay my debt of gratitude to them, to practice the Way with all the energy I can muster, and to repay the blessings through this training.

Gassho.

17

LEAVING FALSEHOOD, EMBRACING REALITY

Rev. Setsujo Uchiyama

ON NEW YEAR'S DAY in 1950, I was on my way to the nuns' training monastery. For a Japanese person, there is no other time like the New Year to reflect and seriously think about changing one's attitude. In my early childhood, I just enjoyed the New Year holidays. As I grew, I started to consider the future, and I began to feel that as a person of religion—as a nun—I had to find a true way of living.

Grieving the death of my father, I shaved my head. I was young; I didn't know east from west. Even in elementary school, occasionally on a Sunday I would be brought for takuhatsu to the neighboring town—without understanding the real meaning of it. Soon it started to be unbearable, and I felt that by any means necessary, I wanted to know the truth.

But no matter how many books I read, faith wasn't arising in me, and I still didn't know the way of a real monastic. *If I bow to a Buddha statue on top of the wooden altar decorated with gold leaf or to a Jizo statue without a head on the roadside, will my prayers ever reach them? Is there any benefit in hastily reading a sutra composed of difficult characters?* I wondered. I continued to go to other temples to learn sutras and to help with temple matters, yet just chanting didn't seem like a real way to liberate my deceased father or other beings from suffering, and my anguish only grew deeper.

Finally when I learned I would be able to join the nuns' seminary I had longed to attend, I felt relief. In high spirits and with a pleasant fantasy that finally I would learn the true mission of a monastic, I passed under the seminary gate. But within a year I was faced with the same problems again. *Why did Shakyamuni Buddha throw away honor and wealth and go looking for the Way? What was the enlightenment he attained under the Bodhi tree that he wasn't able to fully express in all his forty-nine years of preaching? Why did the successive generations of ancestors shed their blood and break their bones in training? And given that, why are monastics now only studying, without doing training?* These worries and doubts only grew as I studied various texts and listened to lectures. *If I don't have faith and I am not learned enough to speak about the teachings, how can I interact with society?* My anguish at the end of my fourth year was severe.

As I approached graduation, I was torn between two paths: study or practice. I finally decided to pursue practice. At my graduation ceremony, the other nuns were sentimental and expressed regret at having to leave the seminary, but I was vibrating with hope for the future. In the farewell address, a representative of the students staying behind said, "Among you, our older Dharma sisters, there will be those who will engage in service to community, those who will continue their education at institutes of the highest learning, and those who—with an unstoppable Way-seeking mind—will knock on the gates of Zen training monasteries. . . ." To myself I said, *That last one is me!*

I smiled as I stood in front of the *hondo* (main temple hall), with a wicker box protecting my *okesa* (monastic robe made of square patches of material). Then I headed out for the train station, taking my first steps toward buddhahood. Before I returned to my home temple, I visited a nun who had been to the nunnery in Tokyo. I asked her to prepare all the letters required to enter the training there.

In the evening I reached my temple, and leaving my bags as they were, I went directly to my teacher and said, "Just as I am now, I don't think I have the right to help people. Please let me go to the nuns' training monastery." Without saying anything, my teacher went into her room. She had been counting the days, looking forward to my graduation, and although I was prepared for such a reaction, I acutely felt my elderly teacher's loneliness and my mind was deeply shaken.

I eventually received permission from her to go for one year. I sent in the formal application and waited. I was finally accepted, and as my departure day grew closer, my teacher's sadness increased. It was heartrending, but I steeled my heart and concentrated on preparations, not deviating from my aim.

The day of departure for Tokyo came at last. Looking at my hometown from the train, I recalled the words of a person of old vowing, "If I won't finish my practice, I won't return."[34] I, too, vowed, *Until I attain the one real thing that will allow me to stand before people as a person of religion with true confidence, I will absolutely not set foot on the soil of my hometown again.*

I had never seen Tokyo, and its brilliance was like a dream, but my mind was set; I went directly to the temple.

At the front gate, full of emotion and nervousness, I hit the han. After a while, a nun came out. I had been told that I would be asked questions at the entrance, but I didn't know what I would be asked, nor what would happen if I didn't reply well. Most likely the waiting and questioning took just a short while, but to me it felt as if it were three long years.

After I entered, it was time for tangazume, where I had to do zazen for three days before training could begin. I was cautioned not to talk to anyone or break my posture. I sat, thinking nervously, *After overcoming all that opposition from my teacher, if I were to be sent out for having a bad attitude during tangazume, how could I face my teacher again?* To me, the strangest thing about this practice place, which I had heard was so strict, was the silence—not a sound could be heard. It felt deeply peaceful.

However, sitting for three days paying attention to correct posture, in a place I knew no one, was really difficult. I took it as a punishment for being so spoiled at home, and the boredom of it made me wholeheartedly repent. Then the long, long three days finished and finally I was formally allowed to enter the training.

What I was taught by the Venerable Abbess—and everything I saw and heard—was as different from the religion that I had known until then as heaven is from earth. The hardship of sesshin was beyond words, but when I saw the attitude of other nuns earnestly searching for the truth, I remembered: *Since childhood, I have been looking to resolve this mysterious anguish of mind, and the key to this resolution is in zazen.* Then the hardship became something enjoyable. Many times, in gratitude for being destined to become a monastic, I exclaimed silently, *I am so glad I am a nun!* Even without having awakened, after each sesshin ended, I felt as if the dirt of my mind had been partially washed away, and the vow to continue without fail welled up in me.

One day, when rohatsu was drawing near, I read articles written by people who had had kensho. Everyone who had attained kensho had been deadly serious about their practice. *Why am I not so earnest?* I asked, impatient with myself. Right then, the Venerable Abbess returned from sesshin in Niigata, and she told us that there were four people who had had kensho there. This lit a fire under my feet.

When the long-awaited rohatsu sesshin started, I practiced

steadily. I was staring into *Mu* intently, but I was scolded, "If you won't give more, it will be useless." I thought that the Abbess meant my voice, so I started to intone louder, but again I was told, "It is still superficial." I had heard that you must go to the very limit; that's where the real practice starts. *Where is this place of the very limit?* I wondered. Eventually I realized that koan practice is not about the voice but about the mind. It was already the evening of the third day.

On the fourth and fifth day I was still prone to doing the practice only with my voice, so I kept pressing myself, thinking, *It is mind. It is mind.* It was easy to just stay where I was. I knew that this world was just a dream and that if I dove daringly to the bottom of hell, there would be a timeless indestructible Pure Land there— but I was unable to make the dive. Even when I was told, "You lack faith. Your mind of seeking-the-truth is not thorough!" I was unable to do anything about it. Sometimes I would be scolded, sometimes I would be encouraged, but my strength would always come back after dokusan, and I kept practicing.

My precepts teacher had never used even one harsh word. I was raised with love, and I had never received a real scolding. Now my ears were flooded with harsh words and unbearable whippings, and my shoulders were hit with the kyosaku as if to break them. My skin turned purple and swollen to the point that if I would make the slightest move with my right arm, I would feel pain. How many times did I think, *Ah, this is too tough! Maybe I should run away and go back to my temple. There I would be greeted by my gentle teacher extending both hands.* But each time I would answer myself, *You coward! Did you forget your vow for when you left your hometown? Will you throw away your great vow life after life, world after world, just because of this temporary hardship?* With spirit I would again face *Mu*, then yet again I would get unsteady.

I was urged, "Don't think you can do this only with your own strength! Entreat buddhas and ancestors, all buddhas of the three worlds are supporting you!" Hearing that, suddenly I remembered and prayed, *Namu Kanzeon Bodhisattva*. But still I was unable to energetically do *Mu* from the bottom of my heart. While I was a person of religion, I didn't have faith. I prayed to be able to practice *Mu* thoroughly, to be able to entreat Kannon Bodhisattva and the Buddha wholeheartedly. "Where did you leave *Mu* before coming here? Well! What is *Mu* then?" asked the Abbess. "I don't know, I don't know," I replied. "It is no good not knowing forever!" she would say. But even when pressed I was unable to answer. It was so hard.

As I was going to my seat after morning chanting one day, a nun pulled me by the sleeve into the corridor. She showed me a cup full of water and handed it to me, saying, "This is the water of *Rishubun* that Roshi blessed for you. After worshipping Buddha, drink it." I was unable to stop the tears that spontaneously fell down my cheeks while I hung my head. I raised the water reverently above my head and drank it. *Although I was so insincere, the Venerable Abbess had prepared this for me. It must be the same as the great compassion of Shakyamuni Buddha, who was careful not to harm even a single bug. If I waste this kindness, I will fall into such a depth of great sin, I won't be able to get out for my whole life*, I thought.

During breakfast, I didn't know whether I had the porridge or not, or what pickles were served. *I should penetrate Mu, penetrate faith*, I thought over and over, practicing and practicing until finally *Mu* penetrated me. When the last bell of the meal rang— *ding!*—I broke through, thanks to nothing else but the divine protection of the buddhas and ancestors.

It is Mu! It is Mu! I was unable to suppress *Mu* from gushing forth. I tried to do free sitting after the meal, but I was unable to sit still because of the joy. I went outside and stood before the statue of Vairocana Buddha, and I saw the statue smiling. *Ah, he is also happy for me*, I thought. Not only Vairocana Buddha, but the pine tree, electric cable, the roof—everything glimmered vividly, bathed in the great sunlight of the morning. Under my feet the gingko leaves, grass, and pebbles, all shining, whispered, "*Mu-, Mu-, Mu-*." The very path to the dokusan I had previously taken with my legs shaking from fear, I walked now with cheerful and light steps. *What can I say to clearly express this joy?* As soon as I saw the Venerable Abbess's face I knew: *Of course I don't need to say anything—the Venerable Abbess sees everything!*

How deep was the affection on the Venerable Abbess's face! My body and mind were so light I felt naked and wanted to shout at the top of my lungs about this inexpressible feeling. I wanted to stretch out my legs and hands to their limits and jump around. When I finally calmed down, I was overwhelmed with a tremendous sense of gratitude for being able to attain this precious state of mind, not through my own strength but thanks to all the buddhas of the three worlds. From the bottom of my heart, I wanted all the people of the world to be able to taste this state of mind.

Through all lives and worlds, I will never forget how deeply moved I was when I was finally able to have heartfelt faith in the absolute existence of all the buddhas. This was what I had been looking for since childhood. My past self thought that as a person of religion, as a guide, I should look down on people as if from on high, giving them advice using many difficult words. But now my body and mind have become light, and I know that helping others means you must forget yourself and dive into the state of mind of that person, becoming one with their joy and their suffering. I must continue to leave behind falsehood and embrace reality!

My mission is to walk vigorously on this one-way path, the Buddha Way, with the continuous, unshakable compassion of the Buddha.

Gassho.

18

WHOLEHEARTED EFFORT

Ms. Moto Yamada

LONG AGO, when I was in the second or third grade of elementary school, I saw in the magazine *Girl's Friend* a cover photo of a neatly swept temple yard and a nun with a cleanly shaven head. She had a bucket in her hand, and she was looking at the falling and fluttering red autumn leaves. I was only eight or nine years old but the impression that picture made on me was so deep that even now I cannot forget it.

Time flies faster than running water, and fallen leaves had been piling up for many months and years. As I was approaching fifty and starting to get close to the life depicted in that magazine, I thought, *What happiness that is!* I said to a group of friends, "If it goes according to our age, likely my husband will die before me, and after that I want to become a nun, and spend the rest of my life quietly, somewhere in the mountains. . . ." They all laughed and said, "What a selfish wife!" But truly that was my wish.

One day while visiting a friend, she happened to speak about zazen. When I listened to her describe the eminent virtue of the Venerable Abbess, I thought I would also like to try this practice.

Yet I didn't know anything about it. I had never read even a single sutra; all I knew were the seven syllables of *Namu Amida Butsu*.[35] I had never heard of the koan *Mu*, and of course I hadn't heard about such a thing as kensho. Just like this, knowing nothing, I went to Chido-an in Nigorikawa to participate in my first sesshin.

There were a lot of nuns there just like the one in the *Girl's Friend* picture. They were beautiful, neat, courteous, and innocent. I completely fell in love with this world of nuns. The Venerable Abbess provided a careful and kind explanation about how to sit and how to practice, and after gyocha, I went to bed in high spirits.

At 4 a.m. the ringing of a bell made the quiet morning air tremble. I jumped to my feet, put away my futon, put up my hair, and washed my face. Although there was no time to take a breath, when I went to the zendo, there were already people sitting there. I joined them, facing the paper screen. As I sat, there was no end to the idle thoughts that appeared one after another. I have sent two of my children off to the battlefield. My younger son, a student of economics at Kyoto Imperial University, was taken into the military in the first draft of students. My oldest son was taken in a first batch of cadets after graduating from the Department of Philosophy of the Tokyo Humanist and Science University. Fortunately both returned safely and told me about the chaotic and grueling army life. I sat there recalling their hardships.

Everyone around me faced a wall or a screen and, with open eyes, were eagerly doing their practice—*Mu-, Mu-, Mu-!* I was trying to imitate them, but my legs hurt unbearably, so I wasn't in the mood for yelling. The only thing I could focus on was how to avoid this pain. I was thinking, *If this is the pain after only a day or two, if I continue for one week, I might end up with my bones twisted.* But strangely, with the passing of the days, the pain in my legs disappeared and I was continuously shedding tears of repentance for all the limitless past.

I was told to stop the practice of breath counting and was given *Mu.* I thought I would pass it after my first answer, but when I went to dokusan, I was surprised. Not after one, not after two, not after dozens of times—finally I had no words left. I realized there are limits to what we think in our small heads and that when we complicate things in our minds, we get absolutely nowhere. There is no other way but to rely on the gods' and buddhas' protection. There is no need to think anything but *Mu,* I realized; logic won't do it, explanation won't do it. *Okay, I should start from zero,* I thought. But when I finally realized that I should be like a white sheet of blank paper, it was already the end of sesshin. Encouraged by Ms. Nakayama, one of the senior practitioners, I made the resolve that at the next sesshin, I really would start afresh.

At the start of the next sesshin, I was assigned a seat right in front of the Venerable Abbess. *Surely the breath of the Venerable Abbess would reach my place, without anything hindering it,* I thought. But I felt too unworthy to sit close to her, so I moved my seat about six inches to the left and earnestly gave my all to *Mu-, Mu-, Mu-!* My head was completely empty, and although I was saying *Mu,* there was nothing there. Strangely, the idle thoughts didn't appear.

The second day finished and I felt hopeless. I was having lukewarm thoughts, like, *After going back home I am supposed to participate in a singing gathering, so I don't want to ruin my voice.* But gradually I started to think, *It doesn't matter! Even if I were to die, I have to fulfill my original aspiration—even if I start to bleed from my throat or tear my vocal cords into pieces!* I stopped feeling any tiredness at all. *There is only Mu! There is only Mu-, Mu-, Mu-*—somehow I started to feel engulfed in *Mu.* . . . I was losing myself in *Mu,* or grabbing onto it, or entrusting my whole body to *Mu,* sometimes drinking *Mu;* or together with *Mu,* expanding into the universe. When the monitor stood behind me, it was like *Mu* itself encouraging me. When I looked at the wall in front of me, I was staring into *Mu*. When a fly landed on the surface of the wall, it was *Mu* landing; when it flew away, it was *Mu* flying away. When everyone went to dokusan, it was a crowd of many *Mu* going into dokusan. *Well then, I shall go for dokusan too,* I thought and stood up quickly, and at that moment I realized *It is Mu!*, and I broke through.

I wanted to see the Venerable Abbess as fast as I could, so I shot straight as an arrow to the dokusan line. There were already many *Mu* in front of me, so I could do nothing but quietly sit and wait for my turn.

How strange is this feeling! How strange is this spectacle! What was happening in me, what I felt at that time, is impossible to express in words. For someone who hasn't thrown themselves into the actual practice, it is something that cannot possibly be understood.

My feelings for the Venerable Abbess are just like those of a baby toward her mother. With love she is teaching and fostering us like a parent who teaches their child to crawl, stand, and walk. And I am determined to wholeheartedly continue making a diligent effort.

Gassho.

19

LAUGHING WITH THE BUDDHA

Rev. Tokuo Ito

IN EARLY SPRING every year, the fir tree in the garden sends out fresh, pale green needles that grow quickly and turn dark green. That tree was planted to commemorate the day my mother brought me here to become a disciple of the abbess of this temple twenty-five years ago. Whenever I think back to that time, my eyes always go to this tree. For all those years it never gave up—neither in the beating rain, nor in winds so strong that would lift stones, nor in the scorching sun. This fir tree accompanied me in my practice, saying, *Let's live a life of meaning as Buddha's disciple.* How many times did it explain Dharma to me, asking, *Can't you see me?* But I didn't open my ears, and I couldn't see—my mind was lost in nihilistic postwar thoughts. Today, however, I can see it anew.

During last year's spring *higan* (Buddhist holiday in Japan), in deep snow, I went with a friend for takuhatsu. The sky was full of fast-moving dark clouds, and a powdery snow was falling so thickly we couldn't see what was ahead. My hat was heavy and my legs were cold. Bracing my heart, I stood in front of a house with a strong smell of incense floating in the air. A woman I took to be the

mistress of the house came out with red eyes, crying uncontrolla-
bly, saying, "I am really sorry, but could you chant a sutra for me?"
Her voice was barely a whisper. *A tragedy happened here. Buddha has
sent us to this house*, my friend and I thought, looking at each other.

We went to the Buddha altar, to where a small box made of
white wood was placed. The mistress's grief touched me deeply,
and my eyes became wet as she told us her story. "Since the death
of my husband in the battle on Guadalcanal, I cultivated three rice
patches and a small vegetable garden and raised my child. When he
graduated from school, he was able to help me. After the rice har-
vest, young men in our village look for more work in other places.
Last year they all went to work for Tadami Constructions. My son
wanted to leave as all his friends were going. I tried to stop him many
times, but in the end he went. In the first week, he was crushed under a machine, and this box of ash is all that I am left with." There
was nothing we could do but cry in sympathy. The mistress changed
her tone, "Venerable, I have no hope left. I have vowed that I want
to become of pure mind, like you, and to serve Buddha." "Pure
mind"—when I heard that, a cold sweat poured down my back. *She
is a layperson, but she has such impressive faith. Why don't I have that kind
of faith? When I say "I am a disciple of the Buddha," what in the world am
I doing?* Feeling an acute sense of my own uselessness, I chanted the
sutras and left the house. After that, morning and evening, I prayed
to become a nun who has a purpose in life.

A few years later, I participated in sesshin at the nunnery in
Tokyo and received the koan *Mu*. Then I went for May sesshin at
Chido-an.

On the first day, the sound of the han energetically reverberating made the clear morning air tremble. With the beginning of
zazen, the sound of *Mu* started, and I joined in at some point. The
Venerable Abbess cautioned me to keep a correct posture. Even
after a few warnings, my neck was still twisting and my legs were

becoming numb. While waiting at the dokusan bell, I decided I should repent for all the things I had done, until it was my turn to enter the room. The Venerable Abbess was awe-inspiring. She sat straight, and behind her stood the thirty-three bodies' Kannon Bodhisattva. I told her how for a very long time I had been careless. I was expecting to be scolded harshly, but unexpectedly she said in gentle words—albeit with a voice that was sharp—"You don't need to apologize to me. You have been careless, and the result is that you have met with the true Dharma late. Buddhas and ancestors are the ones who are crying." It felt as if a needle had pierced my chest, and a renewed urgency arose in me. I wondered what it would take for me to awaken.

On the fifth day of sesshin, the atmosphere got even more serious. The monitor urged us, "Don't sit here inattentively. Don't spare your flesh and bones. Just ask, 'What is *Mu*?' Cut into it, cut into it—cut until you destroy it," and the kyosaku would strike— *Whack! Whack!* One time the Venerable Abbess gave me a terrible scolding: "How are you going to do it like that? You have no mind of the Way." *Ah, what kind of bad karma I have that I cannot become Mu completely!* My tears flowed without end, and a cold sweat poured down my forehead. I was tormented by the anxiety that I could not possibly do it. Just when I was finally able to clear my head, the *Mu* being done by others out loud started to sound strange. Everything I looked at or heard was so strange I wanted to laugh. I thought, *Maybe that is kensho?* I told the Venerable Abbess about it in dokusan, and she sent me back with one sentence: "You have to repent more, this is just makyo."

The bell for afternoon chanting sounded. From the temple's kitchen came a voice that a telegram had arrived. I thought it might be for me, and I went to check. I saw one older Dharma sister crying, saying, "Ah, how unfortunate." The monitor told me, "Tokuo, do the practice for your Dharma sister." *That's right, one day I might get this kind of telegram,* I thought. *Each minute, each second is precious. I don't even know if there will be a tomorrow. As the old saying goes, "If you can't save this life now, when will you be able to save it?"* In a daze, spontaneously, the koan started to come out of my mouth: *Mu-, Mu-, Mu-!* I couldn't help but feel bad for this Dharma sister. Soon I didn't know why but I felt nauseous, as if I had been poisoned. A few times I was just about to stand up from my seat. My head got so vacant that I stopped even knowing how to practice. *What's wrong with me? Am I losing my mind?* Getting worried, I asked the Abbess about it and was told, "Buddha will not let you die. What is happening is because you still have some gap in your mind." Finally the nausea got better and I was able to resume my practice.

At the end of the day, when I went to the Kannon-do to continue zazen, the monitor came and shouted in a thunderous voice, "If you are really serious about yaza, go and sit outside!" My whole body started to tremble. I went out, feeling as if something was chasing me. The monitor showed me a place to sit and encouraged me. The tears were flowing, the lamp on the Kannon-do shone dimly on my back, and my shadow looked desolate. *Mu-, Mu-, Mu-!* I was bothered by the voice of a frog from afar or the chirping of birds. *People of old used to practice even in ice and snow,* I recalled. I went to the side of the well and drew some water while desperately praying *Namu Kannon Bodhisattva, please help me!* I poured the water over myself. I didn't feel cold at all and, putting my palms together, I said, "Ah, thank you," turning in the direction of the Kannon-do. The night was getting deeper, but in the end, I failed.

On the sixth day, maybe because of the night-sitting, my head was heavy and my voice would not come out. The Venerable Abbess said during a talk, "If only you will entrust yourself to Buddha and practice with all your heart, absolutely, without fail, you will be able to do it." I took those words firmly to heart and started over. I was struck with the kyosaku time and again. During morning dokusan, afternoon dokusan, and evening dokusan, I failed perfectly.

That night, I set out for yaza. Time passed moment by moment. My legs hurt. Sleep demons attacked me. Then suddenly, together with a tremendous kyosaku, I heard a shout: "What did you come here and cross your legs for?" This voice was trembling, as if crying. It was painful, crushing my flesh and bones, like more than a hundred blows of the kyosaku. Tears flowed without end. *I don't care what happens. I don't care if I die. There is just this Mu-, Mu-, Mu-! Mu* started to fill my body, yet I wasn't even aware of it—until my whole body was *Mu*. One step forward, one step back, how much time passed? Suddenly, in one instant, as the kyosaku came toward me, I penetrated it. Everything was *Mu*! I broke through.

I had such gratitude for this kyosaku, which was the kindness of a senior Dharma friend. What could appear but tears of happiness? My head was clear and my whole body felt light. I was free. Shakyamuni Buddha and Kannon Bodhisattva were laughing, and when I went back to the zendo, the Buddha on the main altar was laughing too.

Everybody was sitting at their places for morning zazen. Whatever I looked at was dear. *Even such a wretch as me could penetrate Mu.* With joy I hit the dokusan bell and went in. The Venerable Abbess silently listened to me, then she asked me various questions one after another, and I was able to answer all of them with ease. She gave me the next koan and confirmed my kensho. I was overjoyed and forgot about everything else. But the Venerable Abbess warned me that kensho is only the first step in practice; from now on, there is long training and forging. I took those words deeply into my heart. I vow to Buddha to practice diligently and to fully embody this truth.

Gassho.

20

BEING WORTHY OF
THE TRUE DHARMA

Ms. Chiyo Ikai

I WAS BORN in a snowy village in Niigata prefecture, the second child of eight. After graduating from Nagaoka Girl's High School, I was married into the Ikai family. I was nineteen years old. For twenty years I was taken care of by a deeply loving husband and his parents, far from the rough waves of the world. I was blessed with two beloved children, and maternal love opened my eyes and heart of compassion. I threw my life into raising them. I grew acutely aware of the preciousness of life, and gradually I felt I should search for a deeper way to live.

One day I joined the *suiren-kai*[36] organized by Ms. Nakayama and was introduced to Nagasawa Roshi, even greeting her personally at the Niigata train station. There was something in the dignity of her compassionate face that made me think, *This person is a living Buddha*. All I wanted was to be around her, but because of family commitments, I was unable to attend her lectures.

When for the third time I went to greet Roshi without attending her teachings, Ms. Nakayama warned me, "This is the last lecture on *Shushogi*, so come and hear it." I followed her advice, and that one week of lectures was so splendid, so wonderful—I cannot put it into words. The majestic Dharma was clearly explained, and I was mysteriously pulled in by the words that, one after another, sank into my heart. The Way-seeking mind started to light up in me and, forgetting that I was in a crowd of people listening and asking questions, I felt as if I was the only person there. *This is it!* I thought, and I was flooded with the sense of new blood flowing through this dull body. I realized that what I had been looking for all this time absolutely existed. *"Hearing the True Dharma I won't raise doubts, and I won't lack faith"*[37]—such was my confidence.

The next morning I arrived an hour early to the Niigata train station to see Roshi off. Fifteen minutes before her scheduled departure, the taxi arrived. A big crowd of people had also come to say goodbye. When the train was about to depart, with palms joined together, looking at her radiant compassionate face, from the bottom of my heart I shouted, "Please wait! I want to ask you something but now I don't even know what it is!" The only thing that welled up from my frantic mind was tears. Embarrassed, I turned away. My mind was rushing, trying to restrain myself. At that moment Ms. Nakayama said, "Roshi is calling you," and she brought me under the window of the train. "Until October sesshin, practice zazen. Ms. Nakayama, and Daiko, please make sure she won't be doing it without proper instruction," she said. I was surprised at the clarity of her wisdom-eye for perceiving my eagerness, and I was deeply grateful for the blessing of having found a wonderful teacher to rely on—even if so late in my life.

Every month on the sixth, a memorial was held for the passing away of Ms. Nakayama's son and her older brother, both of whom had died in the war. About ten people would gather for the ceremony at her house. We would chant sutras, sit wholeheartedly, and receive Rev. Daiko's and Ms. Nakayama's careful and detailed guidance.

The October sesshin would be the fourth time I was going to greet Roshi, and I was in high spirits. Before leaving my home, I quietly prostrated myself in front of our home altar and said hundreds of times, "I pray that all buddhas from the three worlds and all ancestors have compassion for me. Let me meet with true Dharma." I went to pay my respects to Ms. Nakayama, who was going to join sesshin a day later. She said, "For your trip," and looking at me intently, she took a Kannon Bodhisattva–shaped broach off her collar. She put it on me, saying, "Become one with Kannon Bodhisattva and practice diligently, I implore you." The warmheartedness that she always showed me permeated my body and tears flowed down my cheeks. Happily I was able to meet Roshi, and after an evening ride through fields that smelled of drying rice hay, we arrived together at Chido-an.

The sesshin began with the 3:30 a.m. bell. I looked up at the stars in the morning sky, washed my face, did prostrations, and went to the clean and solemn seat I had been assigned. "You are doing the practice only from your neck up," I was cautioned, and immediately I made an effort to sit better. My eyebrows frowned—there was pain in my chest and my legs hurt. I continued to do my best, remembering my original resolve, but during the morning teisho—maybe because the previous night I hadn't slept at all—I was attacked by the demon of sleep. I felt so pathetic. The spirit with which I had left the house had disappeared, and I was deeply discouraged.

The next day came. It looked like I had been bitten by a bug on my left leg, some two inches below the knee, exactly on the spot that touches the ground while sitting. Overnight it had become red and swollen, and I started to have an intense throbbing pain. I was sitting in half lotus, but my posture became poor, and I didn't have energy. *I won't let it stop me!* I thought, immersed in the practice. *Mu-, Mu-, Mu-!* The stick was striking, encouraging me. Cold sweat was pouring down, and I started to feel faint. *Is this the suffering of hell?* I wondered, pushing it away with all my might. *I won't give up. I won't give up.* I gathered myself together, flying with *Mu*, enveloped in *Mu*.

On the following day, the teisho was difficult to hear. We were told, "Do it honestly and earnestly. If you are cutting corners and cheating, you won't get to the truth." I realized there were still gaps in my practice, and I went to dokusan shedding tears of repentance. The Abbess asked, "Will you do it?" I firmly vowed, "Yes, I will!" And from then on, night and day, I didn't say a single word, I often skipped meals, and I devoted myself entirely to practice. Meanwhile, my leg had swollen like a red-hot barrel, it seemed like I had a fever, and I was getting shivers. Secretly I asked Ms. Nakayama to take a look. She was surprised and worried, and she sent someone to the university hospital for medicine. A kind grandmother quickly went to pick some chameleon plant on the other side of the bridge, roasted it, and made a poultice for me. The next day Mrs. Uchida's daughter ran in the rain to get me a penicillin shot and some antibiotics. Everybody's silent concern and the blessing of their kindness hit me stronger than one hundred strikes of the kyosaku.

The next day, no matter how I tried, I didn't have energy. My throat was swollen and I couldn't make a sound. I went to dokusan, saying, "I can't do it." The Abbess said, "This self-made dualistic opposition will die with just one more blow. When you climb Mount Fuji, the most difficult spot is just before the summit. From the bottom of your belly, *Mu-, Mu-, Mu-!* Keep staring into it." I held on to every word, praying to the buddhas of the three worlds and Kannon Bodhisattva, and I sat desperately. When I heard the sound of a bell—*gon, gon, gon*—instantly I realized, *This "me" who is practicing, this is Buddha!* As soon as I thought that, a waterfall of tears started to flow. I ran into the toolshed at the end of the garden and I cried and cried, my tears filling the whole heaven and earth.

Strangely, after that I was refreshed and my body straightened out, as if a pole was inside me. When I sat, I was like a great mountain—no matter how often the kyosaku would strike, I wouldn't move the slightest bit. I was more and more calm, and more and more clear. When I silently stared into *Mu*, I could vividly hear the sound of raindrops falling, the wind passing through the leaves on the trees, someone walking outside at night, and a faraway rooster crowing. In the garden at dawn, the tips of the leaves glistened with the light reflected in the dew; each drop contained the entire sun. *Ah, what a wonderful view, how magnificent, how wide—it's all Mu. Like a great ocean, everything is Mu*, I thought, and from the bottom of my belly, tears naturally welled up.

I went to dokusan. I was told, "Break through this last shell!" But I was at a loss, and standing on the path to the toilet, I saw Ms. Nakayama. I grabbed her, saying, "You are *Mu*, I am *Mu*, this is *Mu*, and that is *Mu*. But still, that's not it?" She just bowed in gassho and swiftly escaped from my grip.

On the last day, I was driven into a corner. In my desperate ear I heard, "There is *Mu*," and just as I was lightly hit by the kyosaku, at that moment I fully got *Mu*!—I broke through.

All the three worlds, all the buddhas, Mu is right here! Embraced in this thought, I bowed repeatedly many times. There were no tears coming out anymore. *If I won't have this recognized now, even before Roshi, I won't retreat one step*, I thought. Breathing fire and limping, I went to dokusan. The joy I felt when the Venerable Abbess confirmed my kensho is not something I'm likely to feel again in this lifetime. The delight of it truly cannot be expressed in words.

The joy of being worthy of the true Dharma is boundlessly vast and deep. This newborn disciple of the Buddha is so deeply grateful for the blessing of Buddha—and of Roshi. I aspire not to neglect my daily life, not to waste it, to be a good wife and a good mother, to strongly continue to grow, and to be a person of true virtue.

Gassho.

*Sozen Nagasawa Roshi (seated) with sangha members
at Kannon-ji temple in the late 1930s.*

21

LONG ROAD TO PEACE

Rev. Gyokusen Tanimori

WHEN I WAS A CHILD in elementary school, if I was alone in a quiet place, I would wonder, *Why am I living in this world?* My eyes could see, my ears could hear, I could talk, I had a mouth; all of that seemed strange to me. I acutely felt the strangeness of reality and of myself, and it was unbearable at times. But also during those times, I was kind to everyone. As I grew older, I spent my days constantly learning, and I forgot about this unsolvable puzzle.

Around the time I graduated from a girls' school, my daily life started to feel unsatisfying. Day after day, working, eating, giving birth to children, raising them, growing old, and dying—I couldn't help but dwell on how mundane it all felt. I wondered, *There must be some great path that fulfills the purpose of human life. . . . Where is a life truly worth living?* What my parents were telling me was just standard life advice, and I couldn't rely on it. I searched for someone who could understand my problem, who I could clearly trust and follow. I was so lonely I often cried. Knowing that there were likely other people in the world who were also in this kind of anguish, I cried even more. *Maybe the meaning of human life can be discovered by making effort spiritually and going through hardship?* I wondered. *Surely that must be it!*

Finally I was introduced to the nunnery in Mitaka and allowed to take part in sesshin as a layperson. I was twenty-five years old and unable to think about anything else but the anxiety of entering this unfamiliar nunnery, not knowing what kind of ascetic practices were waiting there for me.

During the first days of sesshin, when I was counting my breath, I didn't experience any major change in my mind, nor did I know the taste yet of earnest zazen practice. On the third day, I received the koan Joshu's *Mu*. I felt that unless I could master *Mu*, I wouldn't be able to resolve the mysteries that had troubled me in my childhood, nor would I find out the purpose of human life. I was anxious to discover *Mu* as fast as possible, and it was becoming unbearably painful.

But would someone like me be able to do it? From the start, I had received this teaching from the Venerable Abbess: "Shakyamuni Buddha said that even if the earth were to fall away from under someone's feet, there is no one who cannot awaken." So it is certain that one can awaken, but achieving it might be in the far-off future. *How long will this suffering continue?* I wondered. After ambitiously thinking that I wanted to go through serious hardships, when I was now confronted with them, I shook and trembled. My shallowness and contradictoriness was exposed before heaven and earth, and I was embarrassed. *Mu is the truth of the universe. The truth is straightforward and natural. Searching for this truth, one must confess everything and make one's mind totally honest. Please may I become obedient and pure like a white sheet of paper*: I was praying to the Buddha with all my might. It was the very first time in my life that I sincerely implored the Buddha.

One after another, I remembered all the times in the past when I had thought ill of others, made a fool of others, or been disobedient to my parents. The tears of repentance welled up like a fountain. This was also the first time in my life I cried with my whole body.

Then I started to give rise to delusional ideas, thinking, *Maybe there is some other way, like through ascetic practice, through the physical body?* In dokusan I asked, "Is there no other way than zazen?" "No, there is absolutely no other way than zazen," the Venerable Abbess's strong voice resounded in my mind, and I felt the seriousness of it. *There must have been a time when the Venerable Abbess was suffering just like I am, but she attained profound enlightenment and now is guiding people who are struggling with this great matter. How noble she is!* I bowed to the Venerable Abbess and the great work she was doing.

Mu-, Mu-, Mu-! I had the feeling that there was nothing but *Mu*; only *Mu* doing *Mu*. While still not exhausting the tears of repentance, I went to the last dokusan of the sesshin. I firmly vowed to practice *Mu* thoroughly until I penetrated it. I was so grateful and so moved to have met with a teacher with whom to investigate this great matter.

Sesshin finished and I went to bed, but I couldn't sleep, so I went to sit outside. My body and mind felt perfectly clear and refreshed. The next morning, when I bowed to the main Buddha altar, when I stood up again, the whole universe had become like a white sheet of paper. In that moment I forgot myself. Whatever I saw looked very intimate, like Buddha. When I walked, it felt as if I were stepping on the Buddha, and I was sorry and I walked very gently. Whatever I was told by someone, I would not get angry at all. If a person talked ill of me, I would just think that they must be suffering—I was full of pity and wanted to hug them. While doing one job or the other, I didn't have to use my head at all, and I simply worked with enjoyment. I even thought that maybe I had become a buddha; I had changed so completely from how I used to be. I was grateful for the person who had introduced me to this place, and I was filled with a warm sense of gratitude for my parents, whose deep faith made this karmic affinity with the true Dharma possible.

Then the season of rest between two ango came. I stayed behind while the others went for takuhatsu, and with gratitude I worked. But the joy I felt didn't last forever, and before I knew it, my state of mind started to quickly change again. I knew I had to discover the real *Mu*, the *Mu* of unperturbed peace of mind. So while eating, dressing, talking, or listening, I was single-mindedly looking for *Mu*—there was nothing outside of this search. I fasted, and secretly I went out to do night sitting. Just hearing the word *awakening* I felt pain, as if something was boiling in my belly. Each sesshin I came to the verge of death, but this deeply sinful self was in no way able to be saved.

Three years passed. My parents were opposed to me being in a monastery indefinitely. Roshi was continuously extending her helping hand to me, and thanks to her support, I went to study Chinese medicine at a doctor's office in Asakusa. Since I had to leave the side of this warm Roshi, I began offering incense before her picture, and this became the greatest joy for me. She always looked as if she were glaring at me in reprimand.

I was studying with all my might, and I got my license quickly. When I practiced acupuncture, I became the needle and it easily entered each person's body. Gratitude welled up in me as I believed it was also thanks to zazen. I could not forget about the Venerable Abbess and the nunnery, and my vow to awaken never left me. Whenever I would read the published accounts of other people's awakenings in the *Mahayana Zen* magazine, I would bow several times, and I would cry alone. There were many nights I was so sad that my pillow was wet from tears.

Around seven years passed, until in May, right in the middle of the Great War, I decided to devote my whole life to practice. On the twenty-fourth, the day of Jizo Bodhisattva, the Venerable Abbess shaved my head and I became a monastic, a disciple of the Buddha, someone who continues to practice single-mindedly.

Each sesshin I was in high spirits, thinking, *This is the sesshin when I will do it!* But when the sesshin started, I was unable to give it my all. It was painful to see myself failing like this. *How much in the past I must have hindered other people's practice, how deep the transgressions I must have committed!* I thought. *"Although my past evil karma has greatly accumulated, indeed being the cause and condition of obstacles in practicing the Way, may all buddhas and ancestors who have attained the Buddha Way be compassionate to me and free me from karmic effects, allowing me to practice the Way without hindrance. May they share with me their compassion, which fills the boundless universe with the virtue of their enlightenment and teachings."*[38] I held on to the chanting of this sutra as if it were a lifeline. *How can I become truly earnest?*

Many times I went out to sit in front of the Vairocana Buddha statue until dawn, and when coming back, seeing the entrance gate, I would remember the main altar with Kannon Bodhisattva and my body would get tense. I would ask myself, *Do you have a right to enter this gate? This is a place only for those who have completely given their lives to Buddha. Are you ready to die for kensho?* Then I would reply, *Yes, I will do it until the end. Please let me enter.* I felt as if something cut through me when I asked and replied to myself in this way, but my body still felt heavy, like a thousand pounds of iron. All the nuns and laypeople were one after another having splendid kensho, yet I couldn't do it. I had no trust, no warmth in my heart, but I wanted so much to realize the Buddha-mind.

Ten years had passed since I became a nun. During those long months and days, sometimes I received a gentle urging, sometimes a severe one. But the one that sunk into my mind the most was this: "It is because you cannot bow your head before the Buddha, the gassho you are doing is fake!" *Is there anything more deplorable than a Buddha's disciple who cannot bow her head to Buddha? How disgraceful I am!* I was so angry with myself that I wanted to tear my body apart. Even though I was following Roshi's teachings, making 108 prostrations to the Kannon statue, and praying, my state of mind through those long ten years was just like taking one step forward, one step back. My body and spirit were exhausted, and I was very forgetful, at times even unable to say the names of the Dharma friends I was living together with. They were constantly with all their might consoling me, advising me and pitying me, and a sense of accumulating a great debt of gratitude would fill my eyes with tears. Even worse, Roshi was making so much effort over me that it was probably shortening her lifetime. When I would wake up in the middle of the night to go to the toilet, I would hear a voice, piercing my heart like a spear, *You are taking it easy while not having kensho.* The hair on my whole body would stand on end. I felt as if I were deceiving all heaven and earth. When we went for takuhatsu, I would feel sick, unable to chant the sutra. *While I am the Buddha's disciple who is supposed to save sentient beings, I am just bothering everyone. What a pitiful existence I have!* When my Dharma friends were cheerful, talking and laughing, I couldn't laugh with them. Whenever we would have formal tea, the topic of kensho would always come up. Those gatherings were more painful than anything else. I was the only person there who looked as if her face was eaten up by worms, and I was unpleasant for everyone to be around during those precious meetings.

During May sesshin, Myozen had kensho. In September, Etsujo had kensho. In the end, I was the only person left behind—there was no one else who was struggling together with me. All the eyes in the nunnery were looking at me. I didn't like Roshi to see my face, and day after day I shrank and shook. Dharma friends made Jizo Bodhisattva stamps and threw them into the water, wishing for my awakening. Someone did a seven-day fast and offered the merit of that to me. One practitioner from Niigata went for pilgrimage to the Ise Shrine,[39] praying, *Please, let Gyokusen have kensho.*

Finally the rohatsu sesshin of 1953 came. I felt that if I didn't do it this time, I would not be able to stay at the nunnery. *This is my last chance in this life,* I thought.

When I was washing my face, one Dharma friend told me, "This time you will do it. Don't let go of *Mu* even for one instant and hold on tightly to the Buddha." Those precious words penetrated my body and mind. I vowed, *Kannon Bodhisattva, I will fight until the very end. Whether I will be able to do it or not, I leave up to you. I will just do it until the limits of my life,* and I went to my seat. I heard the serious voice of the Venerable Abbess, "Everybody, don't get defeated by Mara. Strongly pray to Kannon Bodhisattva." I felt like I was Mara, biting into the flesh and blood of the Buddha— *How painful! In this world only I am Mara, the one who cannot be honest.* My chest was burning with pain, as I prayed, *Save me from this suffering!* When I was coming back from the toilet, a Dharma friend was waiting for me. Hugging me and crying, she said, "Please practice hard." *I am sorry I am making everyone suffer so much. It is inexcusable.* Tears, tears, tears.

Roshi told me to practice *Mu* out loud, so I did it in a loud voice. During kinhin, or during free-sitting, or going to the toilet, or inside the toilet or coming back, I continued. My whole body and mind were becoming this voice. I also did night-sitting. During the morning chanting, the Venerable Abbess chanted *Daihannya Rishubun,* praying to the Kannon Bodhisattva on the main altar for my kensho. *Am I not taking Roshi's life away now?* Seeing her hardship, cold sweat poured down my body. *If this time*

I won't attain awakening, surely Roshi will die. Without fail, without fail, I must do it. Mu-, *Mu-, Mu-!* Life-or-death practice, there was already nothing outside of *Mu*. During evening chanting, my throat was completely blocked, and my voice would not come out at all. *Maybe it is a punishment from the heavens and I became mute?* I wondered. *I don't care. Just please let me awaken!*

After dinner, during free-sitting, I was practicing silently when I heard Roshi standing behind me, saying, "Do *Mu* out loud!" When I told her, "My voice is not coming out," she said, "If you tell yourself that, it will really stop coming out. Force it out!" I tried and gradually I was able to do it. The Venerable Abbess, even during free-sitting or kinhin, did not forget about me for an instant. The fact that she couldn't help but try to save someone like me, who lived until today only deceiving buddhas, and that she hit me hard with the precious kyosaku of buddhas and ancestors— how grateful I was, how blessed I felt.

The sixth day came. I was desperately practicing, putting all my life into it. I was told, "Do you think it is already enough?" It was painful, as if my body were being cut up. The seventh and last day was approaching fast, so I made my seat behind a small building on the grounds. With desperate resolve I decided to sit until morning. To the limits of my voice, I practiced. The earth was frozen, the sky was crystal clear.

The wake-up bell rang. On this very last day, without any shame, I went to the hondo and sat. *If I don't do it now, I cannot stay here anymore.* Going to dokusan—I don't know how many dozens of times I was sent away. "Die, die, why are you not dying yet?" "What is that?"—*Whack! Whack!* How many times was I thrown to the ground, but still I wasn't getting it. Tanto, Ino, Tenzo, and Rev. Shudo were all taking turns to sit in the corridor and give me kyosaku. During the noon teatime, in the teabowl I received, there was one tea stem standing upright, and with incredible energy, saying *Mu-, Mu-, Mu-!*, whirling and rotating . . . In that instant—*It is Mu! It is Mu!*—I broke through. The Kannon Bodhisattva statue was *Mu*. Everyone around was *Mu*. I turned around and looked at the paper screen—it was *Mu*. I was so happy I started to laugh. But still I was refused—"Not yet!"—and with all my might, I continued.

At the last dokusan of the evening, I finally received confirmation. I still felt as if I were dreaming; it felt so strange. The Venerable Abbess gave me a kind caution: "Everyone gave you the most help you have ever received in your life, and you made the greatest effort. It was really a small kensho, but Kannon Bodhisattva gave you just the right kensho for you. If you would have had a big kensho, your habit of looking down on people and being arrogant could come up. But even a small kensho, with continuous effort, gradually will become big."

Thinking now about the great debt of gratitude I have for how she guided me—without giving up on me for such a long, long time—I am unable to express it in words. Also, for the sincere mind with which all my Dharma friends were helping Roshi to support me; it must have reached Kannon Bodhisattva. Truly I made them all work hard for so long—I have only deep gratitude for all the Dharma friends who cared for me day and night.

I was able to escape the suffering and sadness of not being able to become one with Kannon Bodhisattva—I was, all along, one with Kannon Bodhisattva. Now I will single-mindedly follow the tracks of the buddhas and ancestors. To repay this debt of gratitude, which is deeper than the oceans and taller than the mountains, I will hold hands with numberless friends and continue to follow in those tracks.

Even such a destitute as me could wake up to the true Way. The joy and gratitude I feel makes me want to save others, as much as possible, from their anguish. True Dharma is the compassion that sees everything as ourselves, even things seemingly unrelated to us. This compassion of seeing everything as ourselves, this perfecting of our virtue, is the very purpose of human life. I will carry on without getting lost. Let's walk together.

Gassho.

Nagasawa Roshi (left) during takuhatsu in the late 1930s.

22

THE ONE WHO KNOWS, KNOWS

Rev. Tosen Fushida

MY FAMILY BELONGED to the Soto school, so every year on October 5, we would hang a scroll with Bodhidharma in the alcove, bring sweets and food offerings, and gather to worship. I heard that in the Zen school, because Bodhidharma was a great person who practiced zazen for nine years and attained enlightenment, zazen is considered the most valuable practice but also the most difficult. From childhood I had always harbored questions like, *What is za-zen? What does it mean to attain enlightenment?* Over twenty years later, a karmic affinity would allow me to experience the hardship, strict-ness, and preciousness of zazen at the nuns' training monastery.

The most difficult sesshin we did throughout the year was ro-hatsu. From the wake-up at 3 a.m. until the end of day at 10 p.m., every day the dokusan bell would sound four times. Looking at everyone's faces, all of them were frightening. I was heading into my third sesshin and I too was sitting with a strong spirit, think-ing, *This time I will show how it's done.*

The first and second days passed while I was immersed in prac-tice. On the third day, at the evening dokusan, I was told, "You are down to one layer of thin paper to break through—if you notice anything, come to dokusan each time the bell rings." I didn't understand *Mu* but I was somewhat glad.

Days four, five, and six passed in vain—and in a trance I went outside. The sky was completely clear and numberless stars were twinkling. The icelike cold air penetrated my body. When I went back inside and sat in the zendo I heard, "You won't have this precious opportunity again. Sit with all your strength." The voice of *Mu-, Mu-, Mu-!* was like a lion's roar. I heard the kyo-saku resounding—*Whack!* Surprised, I jumped in my place. *Why was it so loud and yet I didn't feel pain? That's strange . . .* I thought, and I realized it was the laywoman sitting on the next platform who had been struck. I laughed at myself, realizing I didn't know how many times I had been hit. Sweat was pouring down my back, the time was passing moment by moment, and my mind was in confusion.

Day seven came. *Now is the decisive battle*, I thought. At the 9 a.m. dokusan, I felt a surge of confidence but still it wasn't clear. During the afternoon free-sitting, I came back from the toilet, and when I was tightening my obi belt, at the moment I adjusted the collar of my kimono, suddenly I forgot myself and broke through—*Ah, this is it! This is it! This is Mu!* Heaven and earth at once became bright. My body felt suddenly light, as if I could fly to the end of the sky. *Everything is Mu, precious Mu*—and I made gassho.

After waiting impatiently for the dokusan bell at 2 p.m., finally the time arrived. I went in, saying: "I saw *Mu*." When I looked up at the noble face of the Venerable Abbess—how happy and grateful I was! No matter what she asked, I was able to answer easily.

When the next dokusan bell rang, I penetrated to the very source and for the first time, nothing was able to deceive me. *How vast is my self?* I woke up to the unperturbable original mind and was able to rest in this realm of great ease. Finally I was able to solve my long wish to meet a true form of Bodhidharma. Bodhidharma, Kannon Bodhisattva, and the Venerable Abbess are not something "other." Everything is *Mu.* Everything is Buddha. All beings, sentient and insentient, simultaneously attain the Way; grasses, trees, lands, and the earth—everything without fail becomes Buddha. It is the realization of the magnificent Pure Land, just like this. Yesterday the sky was dark and cloudy. Today it is beautifully clear and radiant with the compassionate light of the buddhas of the three worlds and successive generations of ancestors.

The end of retreat came. On the final gyocha, whomever I looked at, whatever I saw, I was just overjoyed. The Venerable Abbess suddenly pointed at me and said, "Tell us your impression of rohatsu." I was bewildered, not knowing what to answer. But then I remembered the sweet porridge we received each evening after the last dokusan; the steam rising up from it, the smell of this Dharma milk, the warmly rushing blood, and the practice after drinking it intensifying even more, until we were breathing out fire. . . . To express it I said spontaneously, "After the face-to-face meeting, slurping the sweet porridge . . ." And the Venerable Abbess graciously finished my thought, saying, "The one who knows this taste, knows it." The Venerable Abbess always sees through us and can respond sharp as a whip, with complete mastery.

How precious—everyone must find out for themselves if water is cold or hot. Each person has to look for their own treasure by themselves; there is no other way. I was so deeply moved that—thanks to the extraordinary guidance of the Venerable Abbess and to her efforts—I was able to grasp this timeless treasure at this rare rohatsu sesshin on this most sacred day of the World-Honored One attaining the Way. What could it be compared to? I had no idea how I could express my gratitude for that. That was the day when my doubts about zazen and enlightenment were resolved—after all, it was only thanks to Bodhidharma.

I will keep the spirit of Bodhidharma in my heart forever and head toward perfect embodiment, making devoted effort, following the Four Great Vows, helping to create a world of unshakable peace based on the genuine true Dharma. My deep desire is to repay this vast debt of gratitude—even with one drop of thankfulness.

Gassho.

23

SINGLE-MINDEDLY WANTING TO SEE BUDDHA

Rev. Kigai Oyamada

SESSHIN! It was a completely unknown world to me until last September when, as part of my practice, I went to the infamous temple known as the demon's monastery: Hosshin-ji. I inquired about staying there but was told that the nuns of this lineage had established their own practice place, Kannon-ji. However, I was able to have a meeting with Daiun Harada *Rodaishi* (lit. old great teacher). Meeting him was like, for the first time, connecting to the true face of the Nichiren,[40] the founder of the sect I belonged to. Thanks to his exceedingly great compassion, I was allowed to participate in the winter training season.

With boundless Dharma joy and with some curiosity and fear, I headed into my first sesshin. We had gyocha and were assigned our places on the sitting platforms. I remembered one line that Rodaishi had told me during my meeting with him: "If you won't save this body in this life, in what life will you be able to do it?" *That's right, I will do it. Surely I will,* I thought as I took my seat. I firmly vowed to *"single-mindedly want to see Buddha, not sparing my own life,*"⁴¹ and the tears flowed one after another. I had left my own temple four months ago and finally I had reached the place I was supposed to be. I thought, *Buddhas and ancestors have guided me here. No matter what, I have to repay my gratitude.*

On day five of sesshin, I received the koan *Mu.* I believed that if I just practiced as Rodaishi had told me to, I would find my true nature. So although I didn't understand it, I earnestly sat exhaling, *Mu-, Mu-, Mu-!* Various makyo appeared, and I was automatically pulled in by them. Rodaishi said, "Don't involve yourself with anything." The sixth and seventh days came and went. The sesshin was coming to an end, but I still didn't understand anything; I had no clue. At the last dokusan, Rodaishi encouraged me, "Until you know *Mu,* of course you will not understand. It's alright not to understand. Before rohatsu you will surely get it." Lamenting over my worthlessness, my tears flowed without end.

Time flew, fast as an arrow. Before I knew it, November sesshin had passed and the rohatsu sesshin was approaching, about which all the monks from the monastery often spoke. They told me, "Just remembering it makes my whole body tremble." I was afraid all the more as I was still in a samadhi of delusional thinking. I kept wondering, *Why can't I have the attitude like I had in October?*

Finally the long-awaited day came. I had heard stories about rohatsu before and now I saw it with my own eyes. The world was completely white with snow, and behind the zendo people were taking off all their clothes and jumping into the water tank. "*Mu-, Mu-, Mu-!*" or "Sound of one hand"—everyone was trying to awaken. After the last zazen of the evening, the sound of *Mu* continued deep into the night. Either among the graves in the cemetery or off in the mountains, the loud voice of desperate hard practice echoed everywhere. Hearing that, who wouldn't be

Rev. Kigai Oyamada (chapter 23) at age twenty-five in June 1938, returning to her temple after the sesshin during which she had her kensho confirmed.

inspired? Even I, a person of low capacity, couldn't help but jump out into the hail and snow. Before the abbots' graves and on the mountainside, I too searched for my true form.

With the passing of the days, the sangha started to resemble a gathering of demons. The voices shouting out *Mu* grew increasingly fierce. How precious! Both enlightened ones and those unenlightened were coming together, aiming for utmost realization, giving their best in their devoted efforts. I wished I could show this effort, even one glimpse of it, to the regular people of the world. Finally my voice would no longer come out. The only sound I could make was a faint swallow.

At the end of rohatsu, I could only cry. I was full of regret. At the farewell meeting, I couldn't even look the compassionate Rodaishi in the eye and say thank you. In this sad state I went back to my temple. *How good-for-nothing I am. I left my temple and my teacher for what?* I was so overwhelmed with disappointment I couldn't even cry.

After some time, I applied to enter training at the nuns' monastery. But when I finally received permission to go, I got possessed by the demon of sickness and was unable to participate in the first sesshin. *How much bad karma I have!* I thought, but there was nothing I could do. As the May sesshin approached, my body was still unsteady but I thought, *I will do my best to make up for all the zazen I couldn't sit in April,* and with renewed hope I went to sit. First day, second day—I was immersed in practice. I went to the limits of my strength. Day three, I failed; I guess the demon of sickness was still not defeated.

On day five, I was helping in the kitchen, wanting to let healthy people sit as much as they could. When I left the kitchen and was walking around aimlessly, the Venerable Abbess reproached me with a frightening voice: "Why are you dawdling around? When did you become tenzo? Go to the ino room immediately and sit!"

I was completely taken aback. Then, after meditation finished, she said, "Saying that someone cannot do it because she is sick is something a wretched being would say. There is a story about a sick person close to death who awakened listening to the ticking of a clock." *Okay, I will do it. If that's what it takes, I can die*, I resolved. *Mu-, Mu-, Mu-!*

The bell rang for the 3 p.m. dokusan. I went to the dokusan line but regrettably still didn't understand *Mu*. After dokusan, just as I was doing my bow to leave—*Whack!*—in that instant, *Ah, this is it!* My body suddenly became light—I broke through.

I jumped up and was leaving the room, when from behind, in a daze, I heard Roshi's voice, "You are protected by buddhas and ancestors, Kannon Bodhisattva is taking care of you, pull yourself together." Hearing her voice, I came back to myself. I could only cry and cry. I was so happy that I couldn't say a word. After calming down, I presented my insight, but no matter how many times I tried, it was not accepted. I was tormented for over a month while I continued to work on the koan.

In June, I went to Zenryu-ji, where I had a dokusan with Rodaishi and received confirmation. I was filled with deep emotion seeing Venerable Abbess's heart—she seemed even happier than I was—and the tears of gratitude kept flowing. All the people walking on the street and everything around me seemed to be congratulating me on that good day.

When I returned to the nuns' training monastery, all the members of the sangha were waiting for me. We celebrated and eventually the time for the evening chanting came. When I looked up, people were wiping tears away as they watched me. Nothing is impossible—the suffering of people searching for Dharma is the same. I couldn't help but pray that they, too, can enter this bright world as soon as possible.

I need to make all the more effort. I cannot just relax with this experience. I shall go further, toward the unsurpassed Way. Truly I am the most blessed person in Japan. I have deep gratitude for everyone who made me such a blessed person. At the same time, I vow to be strong and determined like the Dharma body.

The thick clouds parted
garden of Dharma in clear moonlight

Gassho.

24

LIFE WORTH LIVING

Ms. Kimiko Shimizu

I WENT TO THE NUNS' training monastery for sesshin three times, but despite my determination to pursue *Mu* with all my might, each time I failed. Even though I felt indescribably good after those weeks of sitting, I also felt an indefinable sadness and loneliness when I returned home without understanding *Mu*.

Then came my fourth retreat. *This time*, I thought, *I will do it!*

Whether I was washing my face, eating a meal, or sweeping the garden—whatever I saw, whatever I did, I only pursued *Mu*, continuously practicing *Mu-*, *Mu-*, *Mu-!* I was unaware of the cold or time passing. Sometimes, even in the cold, I felt so much heat that I would take off an outer layer, then take off the second layer, then the third—until I was just in my undergarment doing the practice, completely dripping with sweat. I don't know how many times I was sent out from the dokusan room and then slipped and fell on the ground in the corridor. Other times, I was oblivious to the pain from the kyosaku and just completely absorbed in practice. At night, even if I laid down, I was unconsciously doing

Mu-, Mu-, Mu-! After realizing that it was my own voice I heard, I would get up and go to the corridor to sit.

Sometimes when I was prone to lose heart, I would tell myself, *Anyone can do it, so surely I can do it as well!* With all my heart I would rely on Kannon Bodhisattva, but even though I was praying and sincerely putting my life on the line, still it was not enough. I would get frantic, then I would again calm down, and thus the sesshin continued.

After some time, the sound of the bonsho began to sound with *Mu* and everything around me appeared to be doing *Mu.* Soon everything within my body and outside it was full of *Mu.*

On the sixth day, when I was returning from dokusan, I heard the sound of the Venerable Abbess coughing, and suddenly I realized . . . *Everything is Mu!* I broke through.

Whatever I looked at, I couldn't help but put my hands in gassho. Everything outside of me—including others' faces—looked so bright, as if resounding with the joy of my heart. The freshness of completely entrusting body and mind to the Buddha! It is impossible to express in words how deeply touched I was by this greatest joy.

Thanks to the help of the Venerable Abbess and all the practice leaders, I was able to attain the joy of kensho—even if only a small one. At the same time, a sense of repentance, courage, and hope welled up in the depths of my mind and body. Tears kept flowing down, unstoppable. I started to wonder if, until now, I had been considerate toward my parents after all . . . and with other people in various situations. Had I truly connected with them? Had I served them with a kind heart? I could see flaw after flaw in myself, and my heart was full of repentance. I wanted to quickly run to anyone I had thought ill of and apologize. In front of the Venerable Abbess and her great virtue, I could only bow my head.

I had had many pleasant and joyful experiences in the past, but all of them were merely a memory resting somewhere in the back of my head. The benefit that my mind attained through kensho, however, is now present in my daily life, always alive and deeply nourishing. When I get pulled about by unimportant things or I become sad or feel lonely, suddenly I realize that I have forgotten about the Buddha and that within me, always, there is a buddha.

All the difficulties or mistakes that come one after another in different forms, zazen allows me to look at them calmly and serves me as a compass. I stopped thinking about how things look to other people and started to contemplate how they should be. I gained the confidence that anything I set myself to earnestly do, I would accomplish. I feel deep gratitude to the many people who guided me to this precious Buddhadharma, and I feel keenly how very lucky I was. I pray that as many people as possible can meet with the Buddhadharma, share this joy, and together live a worthy life.

After awakening, I went to my hometown to visit my parents and help them with their farm. I wrote a letter to the Venerable Abbess, saying, "Thanks to you, I am full of energy. I have completely become a village girl—face black from the sun and wearing farmer's clothes." She replied, "A girl with a black face, in farmer's clothes, walking on the path between fields, how lovely! Everybody here at the nuns' training monastery marveled at how when you came here to practice zazen for the first time, you were a nineteen-year-old naive girl, but you became a vigorous, dignified grown-up." Reading that, I shined with hope.

Gassho.

25

TAMING ONESELF

Rev. Hogaku Shibutani

WHEN I WAS SEVENTEEN, against the wishes of my parents and relatives, I left home to become a nun. I believed that if only I could graduate from the nuns' seminary, I would become a good monastic. My older Dharma sisters encouraged me, saying that the time right after entering is the most important and that I should work hard. My mother told me that the greatest goal for a human being is to improve one's character, so I should not spare a single moment. To satisfy everyone's expectations, I earnestly followed their advice.

Shortly after I entered the seminary, I read in a Zen studies textbook: "One indeed is one's own refuge; how can others be a refuge? With oneself thoroughly tamed, one can attain a refuge, which is so difficult to attain."[42] I keenly felt that this was the way to true peace of mind. If not, how else could the Way of liberation be found?

From morning until evening, I made an effort to tame myself, and four years passed like a dream. Just as I was about to graduate, I realized I had no confidence at all. Although I made every effort to be virtuous and disciplined, I was anxious and my steps were unsteady. In truth, I was miserable, sometimes filled with anger and sometimes so sad I had to wring my sleeves of tears. I felt hopeless and wanted only to entrust myself to something great and infinite.

Suddenly I remembered that when I was in the fourth grade, one of my Dharma sisters had told me she was going to the nuns' training monastery in Tokyo to "tirelessly polish herself in the best place for nuns to practice." I was confident that if I went to this same nunnery, I would be saved. I asked her for help to write to the nunnery, and I received an invitation to come for November and December sesshin. I departed amid the sound of air-raid sirens.

I felt such joy encountering this most difficult-to-encounter true Dharma and meeting a true teacher! My efforts to tame myself had taken me this far, and now I was being shown the way to become a true nun. I saw a light at the end of the tunnel. When my stay there came to an end, I went back to my home temple encouraged and with confidence.

The war intensified, and I was unable to go to Kannon-ji to participate in sesshin, but I kept up my practice. Then the war ended and the state of society gradually worsened. I felt that we nuns should help purify society. I made time to go for takuhatsu, offering the merit to the people who had died in the war. A Dharma sister who had just done rohatsu sesshin at Kannon-ji stopped for a visit on her way home. She scolded me harshly: "Why didn't you come to the nunnery for this precious sesshin? Why are you aimlessly wandering around? Even lay girls are coming and seriously practicing, seeking the Way, but you, a monastic, what are you dawdling over? Get your act together!" Hearing those words, I resolved to do it without fail.

Starting on New Year's Day, I sat one zazen period in the morning, went to chant in the village, and sat another zazen period in the evening. I continued that schedule for a month. The snow piled up from daily storms, but I took it with gratitude as a test of my determination and an urging onward from the buddhas and ancestors. Staring into the black clouds, I continued to fight the blizzards. Walking until late evening wasn't a problem for me—I didn't feel scared or lonely at all. There was just *Mu.*

One time I was especially late coming back, and my older Dharma sister, who continuously sat zazen with me and was a great support, had kept the sliding storm shutters of the entrance open, waiting for me all night. I felt that unless I had kensho, I could never repay this great debt of gratitude. I vowed to repay her kindness, no matter what extreme hardships I would need to endure.

The more I got used to sitting, the more I wanted to do it. I felt I was becoming a great, dignified self, and in this state of mind, I decided that I would like to return to the nunnery for sesshin again. I rushed through the ceremonies for the New Year and, with the support of my Dharma sister, went to Tokyo. I arrived at the beloved nunnery, after a three-year break, on the first day of January sesshin. The Venerable Abbess said, "This time, without fail, get kensho before going back." I vowed, "Yes! I will without fail be a victorious one!"

The sesshin ended. Despite the earnest urging of the Venerable Abbess, I didn't make it. How regrettable, how embarrassing it felt; it was hard for me to look others in the eyes. Despite this, after all the effort of sesshin, I was clearly aware of a freshness—a different state of mind than the one I had had before.

The March sesshin was approaching, but my teacher was sick in bed, so I couldn't ask her permission to go to sesshin. But without resolving this most important matter of life and death, I was unable to concentrate on anything else. In the end, my older Dharma sister took over responsibility for our teacher, and she even helped me to prepare and paid the cost of travel. While apologizing for the deep sin of leaving my teacher in her sickbed, I departed for the nuns' training monastery with a friend. I arrived in Tokyo with a determined spirit, vowing, *If this time I don't attain the Way, I will not leave here alive!* On the way, I washed all my clothes in the water of a stream. I entered the nunnery in the pouring rain.

My state of mind had completely regressed and I was unable to gain any ground. Time was passing quickly. The atmosphere in the zendo was intimidating and the sound of the kyosaku was resounding relentlessly. As the bell rang and dokusan began, I was full of distracting thoughts. The Venerable Abbess offered encouraging words that pierced through my bones and cut out my heart. I shed bitter tears. Although I was desperately fighting, I heard only, "This is just logic. This is only an explanation of *Mu!*" Everything was being taken away from me.

I thought many times, *Is there any worse suffering in the world than this? I wish I could die!* The pain was like having a hot iron ball in my mouth and being neither able to swallow it nor spit it out. It is through enduring this pain that I began to really rely on the buddhas and ancestors. Thanks to that, various steps on the way opened to me and I could advance deeper and deeper.

Each time I went to dokusan and encountered the Venerable Abbess's virtue, I was purified and the moon of suchness of original mind shone bright. As I continued to practice, each breath became more composed, more precious, and I felt grateful.

> The shadow of pine
> Its darkness is the moon's
> Very light

From the third day, the kyosaku was even more intense, and I was flooded with very harsh and honest words, the likes of which

I had never heard before, even from my parents or ordination teacher. *I don't have to go through all this difficulty. I could just be a part of the nuns' world and live peacefully*, I thought, contemplating running away.

During that day's teisho, the Venerable Abbess said, "There is a person here who is thinking, 'Even without all this hardship, everyone will still be friendly to me, I can receive offerings—maybe I should run away.' This cowardly disposition should quickly be killed!" Involuntarily I started to shake and tremble, my tears flowed without stopping, and I was filled with deep remorse. I knew that in a clear mirror, everything is reflected just as it is. If there is a falsehood even the size of a tip of a needle, it is no good—the practice has to be pure and honest. I was trying and failing and trying again. *With only the strength of this small self, I cannot possibly do it*, I thought. *But trusting in true Dharma, relying on the buddhas and ancestors, relying on the Venerable Abbess, I will do my best—that's how attaining the Way is possible.*

On day five, I went without sleep and I forgot to eat my meals. My throat felt as if it were going to burst open. *That's it, I cannot do this practice anymore!* I thought, entering the dokusan room. When I presented my koan in front of the Venerable Abbess, strangely I got courage and a strength gushed forth. "It's tough, isn't it?" she asked. "Your elder Dharma sisters went through one-hundredfold and one-thousandfold hardships." *Even this is so hard, how could anyone endure one thousand times more?* . . . But as time passed and I was giving my all, the limitless *one ten-thousand-mile-long iron bar* started to emerge. I don't remember if I was hit twenty or thirty times by the Venerable Abbess's eager kyosaku, but feeling the blood of the buddhas and ancestors continuously flowing into my body, I bowed.

Soon the sixth day came. I was giving my all, vowing, *This time I will grasp it.* In the early-morning dokusan, I failed. Paper screens were turning yellow and I couldn't see anything. *Mu-, Mu*——the koan, like breathing out fire, surged through me from the bottom of the earth. My tears were flowing, as was snot and drool, but I didn't have a moment to spare to wipe them away. *Mu-, Mu-, Mu-!* Just pressing forward—effortlessly, all body-mind started to become *Mu*. Reaching this place, it wasn't hard anymore. The Venerable Abbess was saying, "It is here, it is here," but still I didn't grasp it. She told me not to rest for even one breath during chanting or teisho or during meals.

I heard that in the morning dokusan my friend had awakened. Supposedly she did it by adding a bit of delight and joy to her mind. *This time it is my turn,* I thought. With more peace of mind, I plunged into it, single-mindedly pushing forward. However, during the 3 p.m. dokusan, I still failed.

I was waiting for the 8 p.m. dokusan bell. My chest was throbbing. I hit the bell, absorbed, and went into dokusan. The Venerable Abbess grabbed my collar and said, "This is it! This is it! What is *Mu*?" I was thrown out of the dokusan room with that question. Although I desperately fought and struggled, it was in vain. Finally I heard the chant "Great is the matter of life and death, impermanence is swift," and I realized that again, the day had passed fruitlessly. Vowing that this night, no matter what, I would do my best, I went out to the forest near the Shinto shrine, which even during the day was dim, and continued sitting. My friend sat behind the shrine and I sat in front, but I was attacked by a demon of sleep. I went back to the temple, to a statue of Vairocana Buddha. *Mu-, Mu*——with all my body I was squeezing it out, my throat in pain as if it were about to burst open. *How long will I be pulled around by this body, this bag of shit? Mu-, Mu*——it was an immense struggle.

I forgot what time it was, and at some point I noticed that my whole body felt cold. *What? I fell asleep here?* When I realized this, I looked up at the statue beside me. *Isn't this Vairocana Buddha, who shines the great bright light on this plum tree, on all the plants, encouraging me, "Do it, do it"?* I looked up at the sky. The stars were brilliantly shining as if they were jewels that had been scattered there. In a daze I started to prostrate to Shakyamuni Buddha. Inexplicably, my state of mind became fresh and light.

The last wake-up bell of the sesshin resounded through the temple. I was somehow composed, and I sat with dignity. The Venerable Abbess's passionate kyosaku was sharp. With each strike her compassion warmly flowed into our blood, into our flesh. When the dokusan bell rang, I was staring into *Mu*, slowly but surely pushing. *Mu* started to well up on its own, and it felt as if my breath could stop at any moment. In a trance I hit the dokusan bell, desperately presented *Mu*, and was pressed with "What is *Mu*? What is *Mu*?" and sent away. I went again to dokusan and was driven into a place of no escape. *I cannot do it anymore. I gave it my all! Buddha, please do something. Whether I get it or not, I leave it up to you*, I prayed. After being sent away yet again, I was told by Tanto Osho, "You should go there with the spirit that with this one breath you will either kill the Venerable Abbess or die!" *Boom!* It resonated throughout my whole body. With all my body and mind, I wrung out *Mu-, Mu-!* I went to dokusan. The Venerable Abbess suddenly raised up the kyosaku, saying, "Not clear," and stabbed my belly. In this instant I exclaimed powerfully, "It is *Mu*!" Completely entering me when I entered it,[43] I broke through.

There was no falsehood—not even the tiniest, needle-size gap in this reality. The Venerable Abbess's eyes were shining, full of tears, and she was smiling affectionately. "Venerable Abbess, thank you very much!" Tears started to flow and fall without end. The Venerable Abbess's face when I entered the room and when I left the room—there was a world of difference. *It is the world of Mu, changing its appearance.*

For the first time I saw that this dear, beloved world I had been seeking, this great truth of absolute oneness, was the very form of the original self. I was beside myself with ecstatic joy. Outside, seeing the calm and peaceful faces of everyone waiting for doku-san, I made gassho toward them.

Only after transcending life and death was I able to fully appreciate the preciousness and blessing of this effort without sleep or rest. Chanting the morning sutras as if for the first time, I could only cry. The heaviness in my shoulders had dropped all at once and I was at ease. There was only boundless gratitude for the Venerable Abbess, Tanto Osho, and everyone. I wished for all people, especially all the nuns of the world, to enter this Way and attain this joy, this gratitude.

It was completely quiet inside the zendo. Sometimes I would take my hand out from the sleeve of my robe and look at it in wonder as I sat there soaked in joy. I was able to successfully penetrate the barrier of *Mu* and take this first necessary step to tame myself.

The time came for the last dokusan. I listened to the advice on the attitude I should have from now on, and I vowed to continue my efforts without fail. Finally, the sesshin ended. Everyone was in tears of happiness for me. My heart was full. To celebrate, we ate red bean rice made by the tenzo, who put her whole heart into it. *Ah, the world of the Way is strict, but this strictness is filled with the taste of inexpressible warmth, boundless vastness, depth, wisdom, and compassion.*

Although it was hard to leave, I headed back home. When the Venerable Abbess saw me off at the temple's entrance, her compassionate face was filled with light. "Goodbye," I said very softly. My awakening had been the fruit of all the blood shed by the buddhas and ancestors to attain the Way. There was nothing I could do but fully bow.

"Sentient beings are numberless, I vow to save them"—the buddhas and ancestors had also poured all their energy into this vow, so we should make a diligent effort to be in union with them. To carry out this mission—reaching up to seek Bodhi, and down to transform sentient beings—I vow to continuously make an effort.

Gassho.

26

BOUNDLESS GRATITUDE

Ms. Chiyoko Uchida

TWENTY-FIVE YEARS had passed since I was married off. Still young and stupid, I continued to do just as my mother had told me—walk behind my husband and do not disturb him. Throughout our life, we couldn't avoid having to earn a livelihood in the mundane world, like everyone else, but we had an especially tough time. We were pushed and pulled from all directions. Just as soon as I thought I could take a calm breath, a great wave as tall as a mountain would rise up and wash everything away. Falling down and getting up, I worked with all my might. Sometimes my husband encouraged me, sometimes he scolded me. I just continued to walk forward. I was blessed with two beloved children; to raise them, I had to keep going. Every day was a continuous battle from which I couldn't retreat.

My children grew up quickly. Both were bright and fast learners: one went to Tokyo Women's Medical University, the other to Keio University. I had a small business, and I was blessed to have employees. If we worked hard with single-minded attention, I was able to manage.

Then I began to reflect on myself, on how feeble I was. *What's wrong with you?* a voice inside would say, and I would hang my head, feeling a sense of inferiority through my whole body. *Thinking that I have any worth as a wife, as a mother, or for the employees who come to work for me is surely just my arrogance*, I thought. At that time, a friend who is Christian said, "The only thing that is missing in your house is faith." So, when the chance arose and a virtuous pastor came to Niigata to give a lecture, he came to visit me. He came more than once but he couldn't save me, and I continued to suffer alone.

Around that time, I saw how Ms. Nakayama had pulled herself out of great sorrow after losing her son on the battlefield. She had been a great mentor for my kids and was someone I respected very much. I secretly hoped to walk the same path as her.

One day I went to Soshin-an in Sekiya to listen to a lecture on *Shushogi* by Nagasawa Roshi. I was also able to sit zazen there for one evening. After meeting Roshi in such an intimate setting and hearing her guidance, I was full of gratitude, and I made up my mind to participate in sesshin in Nigorikawa. For a while, because of the various chores of worldly life, I was unable to go—my elderly father had major surgery, my husband got sick, and my younger sister also had surgery and was in the hospital. *My affinity with the Dharma must be so shallow and my bad karma so deep*, I thought, fighting back tears and feeling deplorable.

At last I was able to go for sesshin. My seventy-five-year-old mother, completely disabled for the last seven years, encouraged me: "I will keep an eye on the house while you are gone. I will do zazen together with you while waiting."

Together with three laywoman practitioners, I went to greet the Venerable Abbess as she arrived for sesshin at the Niigata train station. I was so deeply impressed by her that I was unable to say anything. We drove through the fields at dusk, searching for the lights of Chido-an. Then, together with many nuns and laywomen practitioners, we gathered in the hondo and had the evening gyocha.

The next day, at 4 a.m., I got out of bed with the wake-up bell, quickly washed myself, and went to my assigned seat. The stars were still twinkling in the late fall morning sky. The pure wind was blowing on my face. Gradually the day became brighter. In front of the garden was a great towering tree, its colored leaves fluttering and dancing as they fell. A little bird started to chirp. It was a truly peaceful and beautiful morning. *Worldly affairs don't reach this place*, I thought. I was enchanted, sitting and looking at the garden, and I felt grateful.

The first day's teisho finished and the dokusan bell started to ring, but my mind had gone blank and I was the last person to dokusan. The Venerable Abbess, with her strict compassion, scolded me: "You didn't come here to have fun! You left your sick mother—do you want to be Japan's most ungrateful child? You are at a crucial point—why are you spacing out?!" My happy feeling was blown away. Startled, I went back to my seat. Just then a fly—I hate flies—landed on my face. I moved my hand toward it and my legs gave me an intense burst of pain, but I was afraid to move further, scared of the kyosaku. I felt so pathetic that I was unable to go to the next dokusan. Soon after, bedtime came. Without even thinking about anything, I went straight to bed and slept.

On the second day, surprised by the wake-up bell, I got up. I was dizzy. It is embarrassing to admit, but I thought to myself, *This is so hard!* I had forgotten the enthusiasm I had had on entering sesshin. *Maybe I shouldn't have impertinently come here*, I wondered—the old habit of feeling inferior starting to show its face. *But I cannot go back home*, I thought, so I sat—*Mu-, Mu-, Mu-!*

The day passed and the time for teisho came. I was seated next to the Venerable Abbess, so I paid close attention, wanting to etch every word into my heart. During her talk, two flies landed on her head. The atmosphere was strict, and the Venerable Abbess didn't move even a tiny bit. She was like a great rock deeply rooted in the earth. The flies didn't fly away; they just sat there, still. I stared at them intently and listened to the teisho.

During the next round of kinhin, I happened to look in the direction of the kitchen and saw a servant from my home sitting on the porch. Soon after, Ms. Nakayama came out and the servant gave her a big bundle of bedding. Later, when I arrived at my seat, through the window I saw him out on the road, leaving. My mother, who cannot move her hands or legs and who didn't know how hard the practice here is, probably sent this bedding over, concerned that I might catch a cold. I burst into tears. *Oh, I am an ungrateful daughter, such an ungrateful daughter,* I thought. *Mu-, Mu-, Mu-!* As I practiced, sweat and tears poured down my face. I was told, "You shouldn't neglect dokusan," and it sank deeply into my heart.

From then on, I felt as if the Venerable Abbess was standing behind my back and encouraging me with the kyosaku. If my posture became bad, I would hear the voice, "You are slackening." If I got lost in the idle thoughts passing through my head, I would hear, "What are you doing?"

At one point I was setting my eyes on a small rock in the garden and doing the practice when I noticed that the moss had definitely grown longer than a moment ago. And its green color became more alive. I was moved. *Everything is constantly growing without stopping for a moment,* I thought. A new courage and energy arose in my belly. I went to dokusan and told this to the Venerable Abbess. She said, "Energy is energy, *Mu* is *Mu*." I went back and started over. *Mu-, Mu-, Mu-!*

On the third day, during kinhin, I was able to walk each step fully. When hearing teisho, every word from the Abbess penetrated my chest. As I did my practice—*Mu-, Mu-, Mu-!*—a kind of vibration began to appear in my lower belly. Something was gathering. I could feel it in my mouth and ears . . . *Was it Mu?* I wondered. *Mu-, Mu-, Mu-!* I continued to push. My voice got hoarse. The Venerable Abbess told me, "If your voice wears out, that's fine, continue to do *Mu*." My legs didn't hurt anymore; my shoulder wasn't painful either. I couldn't care less about the flies, and circumstances stopped troubling me. When I opened my eyes wide, looking at the curtain with the temple crest on it that veiled the corridor, I saw it as completely white. When I went to dokusan, I was cautioned about makyo. At one point a Kannon Bodhisattva appeared in front of me. Another time I saw a figure of my father, who had died in June, standing before my eyes. I also saw the waves coming in on the beach behind my house.

Finally the third day came to an end. I felt pathetic and discouraged that I hadn't made it. I was aware of the clock striking 1 a.m., 2 a.m., 3 a.m. While I was dozing off and on, the morning bell came.

The fourth day—I was thinking how good it was that my legs didn't hurt anymore, and then makyo came again. Not sure what to do, I moved my seat to the side some seven or eight inches to be just in front of a wooden threshold for the sliding doors. I put my legs on them, to feel pain again. I chanted *Mu-, Mu-, Mu-!* The kyosaku of Rev. Doshu was giving me courage. "Throw away this bag of shit. Just this one breath, give your all!" she said. I felt clearly this body was an obstacle, and my mind was also an obstacle, and I resolved to throw away this body and mind with *Mu-, Mu-, Mu-!*

In the afternoon, to refresh my mind, I went to wash my face. When I was coming back, I saw Ms. Nakayama in the restroom. With her face full of love, she whispered, "It is okay to relax your legs for a little bit." I replied, "I am okay. The tears are not coming out anymore."

I was finally able to practice well—*Mu-, Mu-, Mu-!* My pupils widened and my eyes wouldn't blink. I went to dokusan and the Venerable Abbess intensely said, "There is still a last membrane left. I am getting impatient. Break through it and come back!" I vowed I would, but I couldn't quite break it. Just *Mu-, Mu-, Mu-!*, *Mu* practicing desperately.

The fourth day finished. The Venerable Abbess told me, "Even in sleep, you can do zazen." I went to bed but lay awake sleeplessly. Ms. Nakayama kindly held my hand tightly. Suddenly I heard a quiet voice chanting sutras. *Was I sleeping? Was it a dream?* I wondered. The surroundings were completely quiet, and everyone's breath in sleep was sounding *Mu-, Mu-, Mu-!* In harmony with it, I crossed my legs and practiced *Mu-, Mu-, Mu-!* with the sound of the wind blowing through the pines. An indescribable feeling started to gradually come over me. *Ah, I am inside Mu,* I thought. The first bird sang, the sound penetrating to the bottom of the earth, and I became wide awake. While I was single-mindedly doing *Mu-, Mu-, Mu-!*, the 4 a.m. morning bell rang.

Day five was the anniversary of my father's death. *My father passed away, but I am such an unconscious child that I cannot even make sure of his liberation now,* I thought. *Mu-, Mu-, Mu-!* It was so hard, to the point that it felt like the end of my life. I was staring at a pillar. *Wasn't even this gentle father of mine able to let go of life? Why wouldn't I be able to?* I wondered. In my heart, I shouted, *Father, I am going as well!* In this instant, the pillar before my eyes burst into *Mu.*

The morning dokusan started. The Venerable Abbess said, "Go and bring here the real *Mu!*" I went to sit again. *Mu-, Mu-, Mu-!* Suddenly the tears that must have been gathering all sesshin began to flow. In the moment I blinked my eyes and opened them, suddenly I realized *Mu,* limitless *Mu.* All the anxiety left, and I broke through.

After teisho, when I went to dokusan, every single thing was the real *Mu*—the Venerable Abbess, me, the pillar, the wall, the ceiling, the paper screens. The Venerable Abbess asked me many different questions about *Mu* and I was able to answer all of them. Then she gave me the next koan. I was so happy! Even when I went back to my seat, tears of joy flowed continuously from the bottom of my belly.

On the last morning after sesshin, with my heart full of boundless gratitude, I went home to my mother as fast as possible. *Let's get back to work!* I thought, facing the great sky and taking a deep, deep breath.

Gassho.

27

A BEAUTIFUL DEATH

Rev. Etsujo Aoki

FACED WITH A CATASTROPHE unlike anything we had experienced in Japan's long history, after the war, everything seemed to be turned upside down. We all struggled to know how to live. In despair, I left the temple and went out into the world, trying to re-enter society. But things were changing rapidly. What I had learned before the war was not relevant anymore. It was like trying to construct a tall building on sand. I completely lost a sense of the way I should live. I looked for salvation in all sorts of ways—working in nursing, doing flower arrangement, tea ceremony, sewing, and *goeika* (Soto-style hymn-singing)—but I was unable to find satisfaction in anything, and I returned to temple life.

In the summer of 1949, I attended a panel discussion on the topic of religion. One lecturer spoke in a painfully harsh manner about the degeneration of formal, conservative religious organizations and their lack of actual practice. In my young chest I felt something intense, like a fire, and at the same time I felt painfully ashamed. We were told that the foundation of establishing a country of unshakable peace is religion. But not knowing a living religion, a religion that could be put into practice—how could I do something as a monastic? I was in great anguish. While forcing myself to resist my conscience, I was wandering, lost, from one dark path to another. When I would confide to my friends about my suffering, I discovered everyone was crying. They were in the same situation as me. *I must somehow become a genuine monastic and save my Dharma friends,* I thought.

One night, I couldn't sleep. When I opened my eyes, I saw my ordination teacher solemnly sitting upright in meditation in a corner of the dark room. For the first time, I felt an inexpressible joy. *That's right! This is it! What can save me isn't study but rather the way of practice. There is only this one way!* I thought. I made a resolution to practice zazen. Remembering the stories my teacher had told me about her hard practice at Hosshin-ji, I determined to sit zazen and wait for an opportunity to go there.

Time flew by, and the long-awaited graduation of my younger Dharma sister from the nuns' seminary finally happened. On a sunny, cloudless day, after praying at a nearby shrine for the fulfillment of my training, feeling both the weight of responsibility and a firm resolution in my chest, I departed from Shinano. My heart raced with excitement to get to the nunnery, to walk this one path of training. I had been so long in the corrupt world, but even I, with my impure heart, was able to pass the hard practice of tangazume and enter full monastery life, where I could gradually be purified.

Then the very first sesshin of my life began. When I received instructions from the Venerable Abbess, I had no doubts and cried in gratitude over their preciousness. But each time I was hit with the kyosaku, I became petrified and wanted to run away. In this way, my first sesshin came to an end. Yet after that, my outlook on life changed completely.

During my second and third sesshin, the depth of my bad karma showed itself to the most detestable degree, and I was single-mindedly repenting. The fifth and sixth times, the path was getting increasingly steeper. I was attacked by a feeling that *Mu* was becoming more and more distant from me, and many times I broke down in tears in front of the Buddha. It was an incredible hardship being defeated for the seventh and eighth times—when I think about it even now, I shiver. As the July retreat approached, I knew that no matter what, I wanted to break through during that sesshin. I wrote a letter to my ordination teacher in my hometown, saying that I would awaken in July. From the first day to the last, I gave it my all—but again it was futile. I failed, grinding my teeth and crying in shame.

September was the month when we commemorated the passing away of my home temple's founder. *If I am unable to do it in this month, that means I have been abandoned by my founding ancestor,* I thought. I was piling resolve on top of resolve: *This time, no matter what, I am doing it!* On the eve of sesshin, a tenzo who always worried about me told me, "Your mind is a white sheet of paper. If you write there 'I can,' then surely you can." I thought, *I can do it. Didn't Shakyamuni Buddha say that even if one were to step off this earth, there is no one who can step off this path? Having become a monastic, how can I continue living if I don't accomplish this path? From tomorrow, without concern for my life, I will enter this great life-or-death Dharma battle!* And my mind became unusually calm.

Before sunrise, the whole Mitaka was quiet. The first strikes of the han resounded, announcing the first step of sesshin to all the diligent students at the temple. I was full of energy, earnestly sitting zazen. One day, two days passed just like a dream. Sometime on the third day, exhaustion attacked my body, my legs started to wobble, and my shoulder hurt with a burning pain like fire. My teeth were loose, my eyes were swollen, and I didn't have an appetite. If I slacked off even a little bit, the kyosaku struck. A cold sweat poured down over my body and into my eyes. But I wouldn't let it defeat me. One mind, undisturbed—*one ten-thousand-mile-long iron bar*—a hard battle of strenuous effort.

On the fourth day, my head was gradually becoming numb and I stopped feeling it. *Maybe I don't have a head?* I wondered with anxiety. I patted it, realized that it was there, and calmed down again. Seventeen, eighteen—the number of kyosaku strikes was going up. I didn't even know if I or the person next to me was receiving it. The throbbing pain in my arm was so strong that even when I wanted to do gassho, it was too painful to raise my hands. *I heard before that one of the senior practitioners practiced until she couldn't move her arms. I shouldn't be discouraged!* I urged myself in my heart, but still it was very painful, as if my bones might crack.

I was backed into a corner, unable to go either forward or back. With all my body, I threw myself in front of the Buddha praying, until we became one body. Each time I went to dokusan, I heard, "You are so close. What are you dawdling over? It's because you are not relying wholeheartedly on the founder of the temple." Roshi's words were becoming ardent, and I was in a do-or-die struggle. Both my koromo and okesa were completely damp with cold sweat. When I remembered that I had put my *kechimiyaku* (lineage chart) and a picture of my precepts teacher into my pocket, I reached in and found them stuck together with sweat. My body was already completely exhausted. After kaichin, I went to the Vairocana Buddha statue, and when I turned around, someone had put their hands on both of my shoulders, "Ten thousand Jizo Bodhisattvas are protecting you. Gather energy and do your best!" It was the voice of Rev. Setsujo. *Ah, so everyone is so worried about me, how kind.* As I thought this, the warm tears flowed without stopping, wetting my sleeves. The day that I had prayed for kensho, when I had thrown ten thousand pictures of Jizo Bodhisattva in the Tama River, appeared vividly in my memory. *Jizo Bodhisattva and Kannon Bodhisattva are with me. Just one more step. I shouldn't lose heart.*

Again, I sat through the whole night. With only three days left, I was on the edge, not sleepy at all, and my eyes were clear. Day five, day six: "Your teacher is waiting for you to awaken!" the powerful urging of Roshi penetrated my whole body. *What a coward I am. Why don't I have the Bodhi-mind to break through this shell? Weren't Shakyamuni Buddha, Dogen Zenji, and all the older Dharma sisters able to cross this last line? It cannot be I am the only one who cannot! Mu-, Mu-, Mu-!* There was no longer any room for thinking about the pain in my arms and legs. There was only absolute *Mu*. I was squeezing out each breath from my body. A few times I was scolded, "You are unsteady!" but I was sitting up straight with all my might.

The last dokusan bell rang. Again I failed and felt the disappointment and regret of missing the deadline I had set for myself. "Just a little bit more. You must not sleep tonight. You will practice until the morning!" The wise words of Roshi, who looked as if breathing fire, pierced through my whole body like a sword.

I don't remember why I chose it, but I made my seat in the middle of a vegetable field. Tenzo Osho and Ino Osho were tirelessly supporting me from behind. This again was painful, as if my body were being cut. *No matter what, if I won't awaken I cannot live. These are truly death throes!* My voice was no longer coming out. I tried to squeeze it out of my body, but my throat was closing. *Even if it is my chronic disease of swollen tonsillitis coming back, I don't care. Even if I were to vomit blood or break my throat open, Buddha is protecting me, I won't die. And if I do, I will be satisfied. Where is there a more beautiful death than this? I came this far and I won't retreat!*

Before I knew it, I was unaware of sitting in the field and of the people behind me; I was just doing *Mu*. When I came back to myself, suddenly, I realized the absoluteness of *Mu*, everything was *Mu*. It is *Mu*. It is *Mu*. Isn't it *Mu*? Yet still, it was shallow. I heard Ino Osho say, "The wake-up bell is in ten minutes. Go back now." *It's already wake-up time?* I was astonished.

Carrying my *zafu* in my hands, I went inside. There still seemed to be some time before the wake-up bell. I went to the statue of Jizo Bodhisattva, and although it was mostly dark, one side of the flower garden was becoming bright. All the various flowers whose names I didn't even know, together they were raising their heads and quietly opening. *I can do it! Surely I can do it!* I jumped up, ran to the statue of Vairocana Buddha, and single-mindedly bowed.

The wake-up bell rang. I quickly washed my face and went to sit. I had just this one determination to sit even for a minute, even for one moment. The bell rang for morning dokusan. I went and was sent away a few times. I didn't know if I was walking or bowing. I was scolded, "What are you dawdling over?" but still I wasn't able to get there. The 9 a.m. dokusan and 3 p.m. dokusan were also futile. With my tears and strength exhausted, I was unable to do anything. Even when I was stabbed with the kyosaku and told, "There it is!"—still, nothing.

Time was swiftly passing by, and the bell for evening chanting rang. I was wholeheartedly chanting sutras as I watched flags fluttering in the hondo; whether my eyes were open or closed, I could still see them. During dinner, as I sat in the tearoom, someone hit my shoulder. It was Tanto Osho. She encouraged me, "You are really that close. Give it your all!" Inside my heart I vowed, *I will do it, without fail, not sparing even a minute. If during this evening dokusan I don't get confirmation, I won't move—even if I am punched and punched. And if after that I don't get it, I will immediately pack my bags and leave. How can I stay in this monastery anymore? I am so ashamed, I am not able to face anyone. There is nothing else left. Just Mu-, Mu-, Mu-!*

At 7 p.m., zazen started, and soon after that, the dokusan bell rang. How grateful I was! I jumped up and ran to the dokusan line. In the instant I grabbed the wooden hammer, I realized, *Everything is Mu!* I broke through. Both hitting the bell and standing up, it was all *Mu*. I went to dokusan. I was able to reply to all the successive questions of the Venerable Abbess without any hesitation, and I received confirmation. I had exhausted all tears already. Not knowing if I was happy or sad, I just sat in a daze. After sesshin finished, all my older Dharma sisters congratulated me. Seeing their happy faces, for the first time, joy started to well up and I couldn't sit still.

At formal tea, when we were eating celebratory rice with red beans cooked just for me, I took the chopsticks and realized that I had a problem in my throat—from excessive shouting out of *Mu*, my uvula had become three times bigger than usual and was laying on my tongue. The next day when I talked about it to everyone, they said that they had never heard of such a thing and burst into laughter. Me too—I couldn't help but laugh at this strange occurrence. Regardless, the joy I had as I returned home was indescribable. If I hadn't been accepted to train at this monastery, how unfortunate a life I would be living now, tragically sinking in an ocean of suffering. When I thought of my old self, who probably would not have been able to endure the anxiety and agony, and might have committed suicide, compared to this completely different self of wonder, of true meaning, starting today a new life as a baby Tathagata—I felt limitless gratitude.

The joy of being in this timeless world that no matter what cannot be destroyed, this joy of transcending death, I wanted to share this joy with my Dharma friends who were still in my hometown. I pray that we will walk the path of the buddhas and ancestors together. *"Walking is Zen, sitting is Zen. Speaking or silent, active or still, the essence is at peace."*[44] How wonderful, how wonderful! The great Buddhadharma is ever deeper. Let's walk the path of actual practice, heading toward the summit, holding on to the rope of true Dharma, making our steps ever firmer.

Gassho.

28

ALL IS BUDDHA

Ms. Tetsu Kondo

I AM A SIXTY-YEAR-OLD gray-haired woman. This year in May, there was a sesshin at Chido-an temple in the village of Nigorikawa. In the days before it, I had been asked by the abbess of the temple, Rev. Shudo, to come and help make the bedding for everyone. There was a person who also came to help from Niigata, and we had a lively conversation about sesshin, and she encouraged me to join them. At the time, I still couldn't imagine an old village woman like me doing zazen together with all those people, but our conversation was so passionate that when I came back home, I remained taken with the idea. I remembered that when Rev. Shudo taught me the *Zazen Wasan*, she had said that even an uneducated or old person could practice it wonderfully as long as they had trust. My heart changed, and I wanted to try to sit.

Around the third day of sesshin, I met Rev. Shudo on the roadside and asked if I could join in. "Of course you can, even if just for the evening sittings. Come tomorrow evening," she said, and we parted. Without being able to wait for the next evening, that same day I went and sat. In the end I went every evening for the rest of sesshin. When it ended, I thought about how there were two sesshins every year, one in spring and one in fall, and that people came to sit from so far away while I, who lived in the same village, had not gone until now. I was filled with regret for not having started practicing earlier.

Again I heard from Rev. Shudo, that in September at Shobo-ji temple in Tsugawa, there would be sesshin and a precepts ceremony led by Daiun Harada Roshi, and that by all means, I had to come. When I was allowed to sit there for half a day, I got to taste zazen more than ever before. I really, really wanted to sit the next full sesshin at Chido-an in October, and I made all the arrangements for the housework that needed to be done.

The long-awaited sesshin came. With the morning bell I jumped to my feet and sat at my assigned place. For the first two days I was totally absorbed. On the third day, whatever I saw, whatever I heard, was so very precious I had to suppress the impulse to break into a dance. Instead I just sat more and more with all my might. Rev. Shudo was always telling me, "If only you will completely, honestly follow Nagasawa Roshi's instructions without fail, you will be able to awaken." So, when going to dokusan, I was honest about how things were going for me and would always return empowered. However, when I held my hands as I was instructed, it felt too slow going. Without realizing it, I clenched them tightly into fists and, forgetting myself, I kept shouting *Mu-, Mu-, Mu-!*

Then came the day of Bodhidharma, whom I worship, and also the anniversary of the death of a previous abbess of Chido-an. I resolved that without fail, I will show them that I can do it, and I gave it my all. Sitting like this with all my might, suddenly, I understood that myself, the Buddha, paper screens, dogs, cats, horses, fields, and mountains—anything and everything was inside this one circle. I felt so grateful that in the middle of the night I went to worship Jizo Bodhisattva and Kannon Bodhisattva, and I paid a visit to the ancestors' graves before going to sleep. The following morning in dokusan, I told Roshi about this joy, and with tears falling down my cheeks, I thanked her. She scolded me terribly and said, "Destroy this circle and come back!" After that I really forgot myself, clenching my fists and fighting with an inhuman force as sharp and clear as a diamond. *Mu-, Mu-, Mu-!*

The next day, at 3 p.m., I hit the dokusan bell, and when I started to walk a few steps toward the dokusan room, Rev. Doshu hit me on my back—*Whack!* Spontaneously I let out a shout: "*Mu!*" In this moment, instantly my mind opened and I broke through.

I went to dokusan and, strangely, I was able to easily answer all the various questions that Roshi asked, one after another. I was so grateful that, on the spot, I broke down crying. Then I understood *Zazen Wasan* well. *Ah, so I am Buddha. The Great Earth also is Buddha. When cleaning the toilet, the toilet is Buddha. Excrement also is Buddha.* Whatever I see, I am so grateful for it that I can't help but put my hands together. I am truly an old peasant woman from a village and I know nothing. But thanks to the Venerable Abbess, I was able to realize that everything is one and I am its origin. I understand that here, Tokyo, China, Manchuria—all are under my feet. From now on, I pray to treat my family as Buddha, to treat my village and all the country as Buddha.

Gassho.

29

THE OTHER SHORE

Rev. Sogen Saito

I ENTERED THE NUNS' training monastery thinking that if a nun doesn't practice under another nun, she won't be able to do real training, to be completely open, and to disclose everything. As I entered into the nuns' world for the first time, everything was completely new to me. I vowed to myself that no matter what, I would practice intensely and become a nun who could walk in the footsteps of the buddhas and ancestors. *First, until I finish all* shitsunai (koan curriculum), *I will have to conquer any obstacle,* I thought. I prayed single-mindedly to Kannon Bodhisattva for the fruition of my training. I had already had kensho with the Sound of One Hand koan, but as it still felt somewhat insufficient, I asked the Venerable Abbess to start from the beginning. She said, "If you will earnestly follow the study of shitsunai, you will run into places that will make your eyes pop out, and you will have a second kensho and a third as well."

Shortly after, I was confronted with a truly challenging koan, and no matter what, I didn't understand it. It was as if everything went dark before my eyes. During sesshin, it is a matter of course, but also on regular days, I knew I shouldn't miss any dokusan, and I was intending to sit with all my might. However, when at the last dokusan of sesshin the Venerable Abbess asked me, "Were you enjoying yourself during this sesshin as well?" there was nothing I could say. It was much more than just sad and painful. I was consoling myself, thinking that ancestors and teachers also sometimes cried bloody tears and that completing the training was not so easy to do.

Third sesshin, fourth sesshin, and finally the sixth sesshin came to an end. One moonlit night, I was staring into the sky. Although I usually didn't think about it, for some reason, one after another, memories of my ordination teacher started to arise. I began to cry, scolding myself: *How can I be so faint of heart?* Soon after that, I received a telegram that my ordination teacher was in critical condition and that I had to go back to my home temple. I received permission to temporarily leave. Soon after returning, I received a letter from Tanto Osho saying, "Practice a life koan of nursing." *That's right*, I thought, and forgetting everything else, I took care of my sick teacher. After a couple of months, she got better. On my way back to the nunnery by train, I suddenly had an insight: *Ah! This is it!* Being oblivious of the other people around me, I was unable to suppress grinning to myself.

The next morning I went to dokusan and I passed the koan. How refreshing! It was like night had instantly become day. From then on, I progressed gradually. As one difficulty resolved, another appeared. Finally when I finished the *Blue Cliff Record*,[45] I could faintly see the other shore, and I started to have confidence that if I continued on, I would be able to complete the whole shitsunai. Next came the Five Ranks[46] that I had heard was extremely difficult. With each koan, if one is not really putting one's life on the line, one will not pass. Finally I received shiho and felt a deep responsibility as a practitioner. At the same time, when I looked back and saw that a person like me could come this far, I thought, truly, it is only thanks to the buddhas and ancestors and the Venerable Abbess.

In April 1954, I finally finished the shitsunai. A full fourteen years had passed since I had started the practice. Truly I was grateful. Until now, I thought that when I finished shitsunai, everything would be so easy. But upon completion, when I thought about the future, I wasn't just carelessly content. The Venerable Abbess told me, "For now you have finished shitsunai, but even when you put in order all your notes, you have to sit zazen well, more and more." *Truly that is so. From now on, it is truly difficult training. Until now I was immersed in doing the shitsunai, but how difficult it is to embody it. How much pain did the people of old endure in post-awakening training?* I felt like I understood it now. This is the true meaning of the great master Tozan's words, "It is calling even more deep in jumbled peaks."[47] From now on, I am eagerly praying to the buddhas and ancestors to be able to follow those footsteps, even if only one millionth of the way, and to repay this gratitude. If I am unable to bring to kensho even one person, it would be inexcusable.

Sentient beings are numberless, I vow to save them.
Desires are inexhaustible, I vow to put an end to them.
The Dharmas are boundless, I vow to master them.
The Buddha Way is unsurpassable, I vow to attain it.

Gassho.

30

LIFE AFTER LIFE,
WORLD AFTER WORLD

Rev. Sosen Koide

THE SACRED PEAK of Mount Fuji towers far above the clouds. Its shape is like a stern father and a compassionate mother, telling me, *Hold grand ideals, wake up to the timeless unchanging truth, abide by the vow to spread the Dharma, cultivate a mind state like a great mountain, be pure and noble like my snowy peak.* On a warm fall day in Mitaka, I walk on a small path through a thicket. All of the noise of the world melts away into this place, into this one peaceful moment.

Fifteen years ago, in February 1935, I left behind the town of Obama on the cold Sea of Japan coast. As an unsui, I was sent out to attend to the Venerable Abbess who was still young and on fire with spreading the true Dharma. With shining ideals, we were heading to Tokyo. It still feels as if it were yesterday.

Soon after that, I was sent to take up a post at the nuns' seminary in Niigata, but after three years I returned to ask for guidance from the Venerable Abbess. As I reentered the training, my own readiness was different, and my vow was more earnest and honest than before. I decided in my heart that I should carry this vow through to completion as much as I could. *If I won't attain the Way, even if I were to die, I will not return.* That was my resolution. However, things didn't go according to my vow. Just before reentering the training, I suffered from an ongoing fever, and even though I recovered, the fear of relapsing was a heavy burden in my mind. Although I tried to hold my resolution hard as a rock, the winds of various misfortunes blew and my legs became unsteady.

For a whole year I struggled mightily with a koan from the shitsunai. Looking up to the great sky, trying to read Dogen Zenji's *Hotsuganmon* and entreating Kannon Bodhisattva, I even began to doubt: *Did I really have kensho?* I was whirling in agony and falling into anxiety that I might never pass it. When I finally passed, I was as happy as when I had had kensho. It is always a fight between worldly desires and Bodhi-mind. At the time I had kensho, I was in such high spirits that no matter what happened, I had the energy to do what was needed, thinking, *That's nothing!* In my heart I was at peace, and I really felt as if I had dropped a heavy burden. I was so tranquil. But when I bumped into reality, it was not that easy for the truth I had obtained to permeate my daily life.

When it was my turn to be the monitor, for the sake of my Dharma friend having kensho, I would forget myself and encourage her with the kyosaku constantly while praying to the buddhas and ancestors. Sesshin after sesshin she couldn't do it, poor thing, and at those times, the Venerable Abbess's face was nothing but grave. Looking from the standpoint of true Dharma, all who come to train in the nunnery are patients. And a *shike*—a Zen master—is focused only on giving each of them a suitable medicine, a suitable treatment. The patient who requires a lot of work can also make the compassionate doctor completely exhausted.

But when Roshi gave the kyosaku, she was like a demon. How frightening she could be! And how enormous her labors were. But when someone was able to awaken, seeing their great joy and posture full of confidence, how precious that was! How magnificent the Way! *The Great Way is not difficult.* I felt deeply the preciousness of this body that allows us to practice this neither difficult nor easy Way.

When I had first entered training, I had asked the Venerable Abbess, "What is the perfect human character?" She said, "Earnest, kind, calm, dignified, composed, and cheerful!" I thought, *Ah, how wonderful. I want to become such a person, no matter how many lifetimes it might take.* During winters as a child, I would sit by the *kotatsu* (charcoal brazier) and be silent, hanging my head. My mother would say, "When you are sitting like this, your face is unfriendly and it is hard to talk to you. A woman should be charming. Her smile is her treasure." Although there was nothing wrong with her words, somehow I thought, *I hate that!* I was twice as stubborn as others. I had so many shortcomings and was scolded often. I was hard to approach, cold, demanding . . . I was an embodiment of many flaws. Now I am grateful that my mother gave me the right advice. The perfect character the Venerable Abbess described is in my own heart. The sacred peak of Mount Fuji teaches me what perfect character is. I wanted to become it so badly it was making me sad—improving oneself is difficult to do. *How terrifying a thing is bad karma*, I thought, and I realized that kensho is truly just the first step in practice. The golden winds blow on the body[48] continuously. I became serious about the difficult task of balancing the truth and life.

There were food shortages during and just after the chaotic war. At the monastery we collected weeds, lumping them together with flour, to eat. But for anyone who came to the temple, the Venerable Abbess would say in a friendly way, "Don't I have something to give you? It is during these times that we should be giving. . . ." Every month on the eighteenth, the day of celebration of Kannon Bodhisattva, after whom the nunnery is named, the Abbess would never fail to give a plate full of mixed five-grain rice to each person who came. Of course it was a time when bitter things were happening, but thinking about it now, I realize that thanks to that merit we could overcome hard times and this practice place that has no fixed income can safely continue.

The nuns who trained here at the time of great hardship were amazed, saying, "The Venerable Abbess gives many things to parishioners, doesn't she?" I would always say, "I myself am a person who doesn't have the virtue of generosity, and I was convinced that monastics should be giving the Dharma, and lay parishioners the material things—but the compassion of the Buddha is not such a narrow partial thing. Shakyamuni Buddha said, 'If someone has generosity in their heart, no matter who they are, they will be able to give.' Just the fact that I learned here how to purely give, this in itself is a great attainment."

Many nuns stayed for over three years, accumulating the experience of sesshin, understanding the taste of zazen, and obtaining the truth. The joy of seeing spiritual patients one by one get well and return to their home temples cannot be compared to anything. The Venerable Abbess continues with great determination to offer compassion and gather hidden virtue. She is teaching with her own life, during sesshin and in daily life—heading upward seeking Bodhi and downward to transform sentient beings. This way of being is like a compassionate mother with a baby—she embraces it, carries it on her back, and holds its hand. It is like climbing up the Mount Fuji of buddhahood in a do-or-die effort, for the one who is pulling us upward by the hand and for those of us following below. But the hardships and troubles the Zen master endures to train others are truly incomparable.

To say that the true transmission of Buddhadharma is a blood stream is true; it passes mind to mind and body to body. Overcoming big and small waves, being tossed this way or that way, I was able to some extent to arrive at the destination. Somehow I was able to discover what Buddhadharma was. So is that the end? Far from it! With shitsunai it is like when a student finishes the standard curriculum—they will only master their knowledge by going out into society. One must encounter one difficulty after another. The words the Venerable Abbess said once during teisho touched my heart: to make Dharma enter your flesh and blood, to integrate it into your character, this is the practice that happens the most after finishing the shitsunai. The more we enter the great ocean of Buddhadharma, the deeper it gets—now I see it, and the more serious about it I become. The distant blue mountains stretch limitlessly, mountain after mountain. How can we cross all of them? But the most wonderful thing is that the universe is supporting us with its oneness. No matter how steep the mountain is, how bottomless the ravine, or how thorny the shrub, we can pass through freely with this support, never leaving it, life after life, world after world.

The sky of Mitaka is high and completely clear, a skylark is chirping. The bright green fields of barley look brave. Bathed in the spring sun, they are burning with hope. This morning I am walking in the middle of them in one line for takuhatsu. Figures in the black cotton koromo and wicker hats, with white kyahan and straw sandals, weaving their way through a forest. One can hear the sound of the staff hitting the ground. It is goodness and beauty that feels not of this world. In the heart of each and every one of them, they are engaged in the do-or-die Dharma battle. Where there is great training, the Dharma flourishes.

Master Tozan said,

For whom do you bathe and put on beautiful make up?
The call of the cuckoo urges you to come home.
Hundreds of flowers have fallen, yet the call hasn't stopped.
It is calling even more deep in jumbled peaks.[49]

Gassho.

After sesshin, April 5, 1959. Shudo Sato (chapter 11) fourth from the right in the second row,
Sosen Koide (chapter 30) fourth from the right in the third row.

Nagasawa Roshi ca. 1960.

Acknowledgments

We would like to thank Rev. Sokan Nagasawa, the current abbess of Kannon-ji, for her kind support for this project and for donating a copy of the original book. Many thanks also to Rev. Kogaku Harada for his permission to use the photos, and to Mr. Tetsuji Iizuka, a relative of the publishers of the original book (Rev. Tetsuei Iizuka and Rev. Koji Iizuka) for his permission to publish this English version. Matt Zeppelin and Jenn Brown from Shambhala Publications provided valuable help in the editing process. Rev. Kokyo Henkel helped to identify the sources of some quotes in the text, and Maho Ikushima Sensei provided help deciphering some of the more difficult Japanese expressions. Lastly, thanks to Remko Popma, who sent the copy of *Sanzen taiken-shu* to us in the middle of the pandemic.

Glossary of Japanese and Buddhist Terms

ango—A practice period in Zen temples usually lasting around three months

bonsho—A large temple bell

Buddhadharma—Teachings of the Buddha

Daihannya Rishubun—A ceremony with esoteric elements using one of the volumes of the *Prajna Paramita Sutra*

dojo—Practice place

dokusan—A formal, private meeting between teacher and student

Fudo Myoo—A Dharma protecting deity

Fukanzazengi (Universal Recommendations for Doing Zazen)—A text by Eihei Dogen about sitting meditation

gassho—Gesture of putting palms together

goeika—A Soto school style of chanting Buddhist hymns developed in the twentieth century

gyocha—A formal monastery practice of drinking tea, sometimes accompanied by teachings from the abbess or abbot

han—A wooden rectangular board that is hit with a wooden mallet and used as one of the instruments at the monastery

higan—An important Buddhist holiday in Japan, celebrated twice a year around spring and fall equinoxes

hondo—The main temple hall for ceremonies

Hotsuganmon (Verse of Arousing the Vow)—A short text by Eihei Dogen speaking on the importance of vow and repentance in Buddhist practice

hyakudoishi—A stone placed in a temple, often at the beginning of the worship route, that people vow to visit one hundred times to accumulate merit

Idasonten—A bodhisattva said to protect the monastery and help gather resources; enshrined on the altar near the temple kitchen

inka shomei—Authorization to teach independently after completing the post-awakening koan training

ino—One of the officers in the Zen temple

Jizo—Japanese name for Ksitigarbha, bodhisattva of great vow; protector of women, children, and the earth

Jukku Kannon-gyo (Ten Verses Kannon Sutra)—sometimes also called *Jukku-gyo* or *Enmei Jukku Kannon-gyo*

kaichin—Literally "opening of bedding"; formal end of the daily schedule at a monastery

Kannon—Japanese name for Avalokiteshvara, bodhisattva of compassion

Kannon-do—A hall dedicated to Kannon Bodhisattva

kechimiyaku—A lineage chart document received during a precepts ceremony

keisu—A bowl-shaped gong used in chanting services

kensho—Literally "seeing nature"; sometimes used synonymously with *satori*, other times referring to an initial breakthrough experience

kinhin—Walking meditation between periods of sitting meditation

koan—A form of meditation with a question or situation that requires an experiential answer from a student

koromo—A long sleeved robe

kotatsu—A charcoal brazier in a floor well with a hanging quilt that retains heat *kyahan*—Gaiters made of white material that are worn on hands and legs during takuhatsu

kyosaku—A stick used in monasteries to wake up and encourage nuns or monks during meditation

makyo—A hallucination that might arise during meditation

Mara—A Buddhist deity personifying illusion, evil, and hindrances on the path toward enlightenment

mokugyo—Literally "wooden fish"; a percussion instrument used in Zen temples to maintain rhythm during chanting

Monju—Japanese name for Manjushri, bodhisattva of wisdom

Ni-Roshi—Literally "old teacher nun"; a respectful title for a nun teacher in the Zen tradition

ni-sodo—A training monastery for nuns

okesa—A monastic robe made of square patches of material

Osho—A formal title for a nun or monk who has gone through monastic training

Pure Land school—A form of Mahayana Buddhism that teaches that through invoking the name of Amithaba Buddha, one can gain rebirth in the Pure Land, a realm in which practice and attaining liberation is much easier than in the human realm on earth

rakusu—A symbolic garment worn by Buddhist practitioners who have taken precepts

Rinzai school—One of the major schools of Zen in China and Japan, deriving its name from Linji Yixuan (Jap. Rinzai Gigen, ?–866)

Rodaishi—Literally "old great teacher"; a title of utmost respect for a teacher in the Zen tradition

rohatsu—Annual intensive sesshin, usually ending December 8, commemorating the Buddha's day of enlightenment

Roshi—Literally "old teacher"; a respectful title for a teacher in the Zen tradition

Saha world—The mundane world of suffering and conditioned phenomena

sesshin—An intensive meditation retreat, usually around one week long

shiho—A Dharma transmission signifying a completion of monastic training

shitsunai—Koan curriculum of a particular lineage

Shobogenzo (*Treasury of the True Dharma Eye*)—A major text written by Eihei Dogen

Shushogi (*The Meaning of Practice and Verification*)—Published in 1890, a compilation of fragments of Eihei Dogen's *Shobogenzo*; widely used as a condensed version of Soto school teachings for lay followers

Soto school—One of the major schools of Zen in China and Japan, deriving its name in part from Dongshan Liangjie (Jap. Tozan Ryokai, 807–869)

takuhatsu—Mendicancy practice

tangazume—A period in which a postulant at a Zen monastery must sit continuously in zazen posture for several days before being admitted for training

tanto—A senior nun or monk responsible for training novices

teisho—A formal Dharma talk

tenzo—A cook in the Zen monastery

unsui—Literally "cloud-water"; a monastic in training

waraji—Rice straw sandals used by nuns and monks during takuhatsu or pilgrimage

yaza—Informal night-sitting after the end of the regular schedule in the monastery

zabuton—A mat for sitting during meditation

zafu—A round cushion used for sitting meditation

Zazen Wasan (*Song of Zazen*)—A short text by Hakuin Ekaku (1686–1769) about the importance of seated meditation

Notes

1. Sozen Nagasawa, *Joshi Sanzen no Hiketsu* (Chuo Bukkyo-sha, 1939).
2. Susumu Otake, *Satori Taiken* (Shinchosha, 2019).
3. Nagasawa, *Joshi Sanzen no Hiketsu.*
4. Nagasawa, *Joshi Sanzen no Hiketsu.*
5. Sogaku Harada, *Daiun Sogaku Jiden* (Daiunkai, 1960).
6. Nagasawa, *Joshi Sanzen no Hiketsu.*
7. Reference to the *Nakhasikha Sutta*, also found in Eihei Dogen, *Eihei Koroku*, vol. 7, 480.
8. *Shushogi* (*The Meaning of Practice and Verification*), translated by the Soto Zen Text Project, https://www.sotozen.com/eng/practice/sutra/pdf/03/c02.pdf.
9. Myoe Koben (1173–1232), a famous monk of the Kegon school of Buddhism.
10. In Chinese and Japanese mythology, dragon kings are deities controlling water and weather.
11. Nigorikawa is a village in Niigata prefecture where Sozen Nagasawa Roshi conducted sesshins multiple times a year at Chido-an temple, where Rev. Shudo Sato (chapter 11) was the abbess.
12. Eihei Dogen, "Attaining the Marrow by Bowing," in *Shobogenzo*.

13. A reference to the Ten Oxherding Pictures, a pictorial representation of the stages of practice and realization, where ox symbolizes true nature.

14. Rev. Kendo Kojima was the first woman to officiate during a ceremony at the head temple Eihei-ji at that time.

15. Words of Tiantong Rujing (1163–1228), as recorded by Eihei Dogen in *Hokyo-ki*.

16. Beginning syllables of the *Dharani of Great Compassion*.

17. In Pure Land Buddhism, "original vow" refers to a vow taken by Amithaba Buddha that whoever recites his name ten times will be reborn in the Western Pure Land.

18. A traditional Zen teaching phrase, often referring to a state of single-minded, uninterrupted samadhi.

19. A teaching phrase by Sengzhao (384–414).

20. The first words that Shakyamuni Buddha is believed to have said just after being born.

21. Eihei Dogen, *Fukanzazengi*.

22. A practice of pressing red stamps of Jizo Bodhisattva's image while chanting the Jizo mantra and then, also while chanting the mantra, throwing them into the ocean, a river, or another body of water.

23. A famous pilgrimage in central Japan of thirty-three temples with Kannon Bodhisattva statues.

24. A short practice gathering that includes a Dharma talk and zazen with dokusan.

25. Mumon Ekai Zenji, from the commentary to the koan Joshu's Dog, *Mumonkan* koan collection.

26. Verse often written on the han.

27. In Zen, nuns and monks in training are called *unsui*, which literally means "cloud-water."

28. Eihei Dogen, *Fukanzazengi*.

29. Shizue Tanaka was the daughter of Mieko Tanaka from the previous chapter.
30. A popular name for Dokyo Etan (1642–1721).
31. Hakuin Ekaku (1686–1769).
32. Seven buildings in the Zen monastery are: *butsuden* (Buddha hall), *hatto* (Dharma hall), *sodo* (Sangha hall), *kuin* (kitchen), *sanmon* (main gate), *tosu* (toilet), and *yokushitsu* (bath).
33. Sen was an old monetary unit worth one-hundredth of a yen.
34. A line from a poem by Seikyo Gessho (1817–1856).
35. "Homage to Amithaba Buddha," a popular mantra used especially by the Pure Land school of Buddhism.
36. A short practice gathering that includes a Dharma talk and zazen with dokusan.
37. Eihei Dogen, *Hotsuganmon*.
38. Eihei Dogen, *Hotsuganmon*.
39. A major Shinto shrine in Mie prefecture.
40. Nichiren (1222–1282), the founder of the Nichiren school of Buddhism.
41. "The Eternal Life of Tathagata," chap. 16 in *The Lotus Sutra*.
42. From the *Dhammapada*, v. 160.
43. An expression from a short text called *Shariraimon*.
44. Yongjia Xuanjue (665–713), *Song of Enlightenment*.
45. A koan collection originally compiled in Song China, used in koan training in Japan.
46. A teaching by Dongshan Liangjie (807–869) used during koan training.
47. A quote from a poem by Dongshan Liangjie on the "second rank of merit."
48. Reference to "Unmon's Body Exposed to the Golden Wind," case 27 in *Blue Cliff Record*.
49. Full poem on the "second rank of merit" by Dongshan Liangjie.